THE ANNOTATED SHAKESPEARE

The Taming of the Shrew

William Shakespeare

Fully annotated, with an Introduction, by Burton Raffel
With an essay by Harold Bloom

THE ANNOTATED SHAKESPEARE

Yale University Press · *New Haven and London*

"The Taming of the Shrew," from *Shakespeare: The Invention of the Human*
by Harold Bloom, copyright © 1998 by Harold Bloom. Used by permission of
Riverhead Books, an imprint of Penguin Group (USA) Inc.

Designed by Rebecca Gibb
Set in Bembo type by The Composing Room of Michigan, Inc.
Printed in the United States of America by R. R. Donnelley & Sons.

Library of Congress Cataloging-in-Publication Information
Shakespeare, William, 1564–1616.
The taming of the shrew / William Shakespeare ; fully annotated
with an introduction by Burton Raffel ;
with an essay by Harold Bloom.
p. cm. — (The annotated Shakespeare)
Includes bibliographical references (p.)
ISBN 0-300-10982-2 (pbk.)
1. Man-woman relationships—Drama. 2. Married people—Drama.
3. Padua (Italy)—Drama. 4. Sex role—Drama. I. Raffel, Burton.
II. Bloom, Harold. III. Title. IV. Series.
PR2832.A2R34 2005
822.3′3—dc22
2005007313

A catalogue record for this book is available from the British Library.

10 9 8 7 6 5 4 3 2 1

For Sandra and Eric Wolman

CONTENTS

ABOUT THIS BOOK

ℰ

Written four centuries ago, in a fairly early form of Modern English, *The Taming of the Shrew* is a delightful romp. Many of the play's social and historical underpinnings necessarily need, for the modern reader, the kinds of explanation offered in the Introduction. But what needs even more, and far more detailed, explanation are the play's very words. Here is a servant reporting, in act 3, scene 2, the bridegroom's arrival:

Biondello Why, Petruchio is coming, in a new hat and an old jerkin, a pair of old breeches thrice turned, a pair of boots that have been candle-cases, one buckled, another laced, an old rusty sword ta'en out of the town armory, with a broken hilt, and chapeless, with two broken points. His horse hipped, with an old mothy saddle, and stirrups of no kindred, besides possessed with the glanders and like to mose in the chine, troubled with the lampas, infected with the fashions, full of windgalls, sped with spavins, rayed with the yellows, past cure of the fives, stark spoiled with the staggers, begnawn with the bots, swayed in the back, and shoulder-shotten, near-legged before, and with a half-checked bit, and a head-stall of sheep's leather, which being restrained to keep him from stumbling, hath been often burst, and now repaired with knots. One girth six times pieced, and a woman's crupper of velure, which hath two letters for her name, fairly set down in studs, and here and there pieced with pack-thread.

This was perfectly understandable, we must assume, to the mostly very average persons who paid to watch Elizabethan plays. But who today can make much sense of it? In this very fully annotated edition, I therefore present this passage, not in the bare form quoted above, but thoroughly supported by bottom-of-the-page notes:

Biondello Why, Petruchio is coming, in a new hat and an old jerkin,[1] a pair of old breeches[2] thrice turned,[3] a pair of boots that have been candle-cases,[4] one buckled, another laced, an old rusty sword ta'en out of the town armory,[5] with a broken hilt, and chapeless,[6] with two broken points.[7] His horse hipped,[8] with an old mothy saddle, and stirrups of no kindred,[9] besides possessed[10] with the glanders[11] and like[12] to mose in the chine,[13]

1 close-fitting jacket/short coat
2 trousers that reach to just below the knee
3 altered
4 old, worn-out boots that had been relegated to use as storage boxes for candles
5 town armory = town/local/common arsenal
6 unsheathed
7 straps
8 lame in the hips
9 of no kindred = not resembling each other
10 affected
11 contagious equine disease
12 likely
13 mose in the chine = (?) suffer/ache in the spine/back

troubled with the lampas,[14] infected with the fashions,[15] full of windgalls,[16] sped with spavins,[17] rayed with the yellows,[18] past cure of the fives,[19] stark spoiled with the staggers,[20] begnawn[21] with the bots,[22] swayed in the back, and shoulder-shotten,[23] near-legged before,[24] and with a half-checked[25] bit, and a head-stall[26] of sheep's leather,[27] which being restrained[28] to keep him from stumbling, hath been often burst, and now repaired with knots.[29] One girth[30] six times pieced,[31] and a woman's crupper[32] of velure,[33] which hath two letters for her[34] name, fairly set down in studs,[35] and here and there pieced with pack-thread.[36]

14 equine disease: swelling of the roof of the mouth
15 farcy: infectious equine disease
16 equine leg tumors
17 sped with spavins = sick/brought down/finished by cartilage inflammation in a horse's leg
18 rayed with the yellows = berayed/disfigured/defiled by equine/bovine jaundice
19 avives (aVIVES): equine glandular swelling
20 stark spoiled with the staggers = severely ravaged by an equine illness like "mad cow disease"
21 corroded
22 parasitical maggots/worms
23 shoulder-ruined ("shot")
24 front legs coming too close to one another (knock-kneed?)
25 half-loose
26 part of bridle/halter going around the horse's head
27 inferior (pigskin was favored by men of social standing)
28 tightened
29 knotted leather (cheap, poverty-stricken appearance)
30 leather band around horse's belly, securing saddle/pack on its back
31 patched, mended
32 strap running from back of saddle to the horse's tail and then around under the horse, to hold saddle from sliding forward; not generally used by men
33 velvet
34 the prior owner's
35 set down in studs = mounted/written out by metal nails
36 twine, heavy thread

The modern reader or listener may well better understand this brief passage in context, as the play continues. But without full explanation of words that have over the years shifted in meaning, and usages that have been altered, neither the modern reader nor the modern listener is likely to be equipped for anything like full comprehension.

I believe annotations of this sort create the necessary bridges, from Shakespeare's four-centuries-old English across to ours. Some readers, to be sure, will be able to comprehend unusual, historically different meanings without glosses. Those not familiar with the modern meaning of particular words will easily find clear, simple definitions in any modern dictionary. But most readers are not likely to understand Shakespeare's intended meaning, absent such glosses as I here offer.

My annotation practices have followed the same principles used in *The Annotated Milton,* published in 1999, and in my annotated editions of *Hamlet,* published (as the initial volume in this series) in 2003, and *Romeo and Juliet* (published in 2004). Classroom experience has validated these editions. Classes of mixed upper-level undergraduates and graduate students have more quickly and thoroughly transcended language barriers than ever before. This allows the teacher, or a general reader without a teacher, to move more promptly and confidently to the nonlinguistic matters that have made Shakespeare and Milton great and important poets.

It is the inevitable forces of linguistic change, operant in all living tongues, which have inevitably created such wide degrees of obstacles to ready comprehension—not only sharply different meanings, but subtle, partial shifts in meaning that allow us to think we understand when, alas, we do not. Speakers of related languages like Dutch and German also experience this shifting of the linguistic ground. Like early Modern English (ca. 1600) and the Modern English now current, those languages are too close for those who know only one language, and not the other, to be readily able always to recognize what they correctly understand and what they do not. When, for example, a speaker of Dutch says, "Men kofer is kapot," a speaker of German will know that something belonging to the Dutchman is broken ("kapot" = "kaputt" in German, and "men" = "mein"). But without more linguistic awareness than the average person is apt to have, the German speaker will not identify "kofer" ("trunk" in Dutch) with "Körper"—a modern German word meaning "physique, build, body." The closest word to "kofer" in modern German, indeed, is "Scrankkoffer," which is too large a leap for ready comprehension. Speakers of different Romance languages (French, Spanish, Italian), and all other related but not identical tongues, all experience these difficulties, as well as the difficulty of understanding a text written in their own language five, or six, or seven hundred years earlier. Shakespeare's English is not yet so old that it requires, like many historical texts in French and German, or like Old English texts—for example, *Beowulf*—a modern translation. Much poetry evaporates in translation: language is immensely particular. The sheer *sound* of Dante in thirteenth-century Italian is profoundly worth preserving. So too is the sound of Shakespeare.

I have annotated prosody (metrics) only when it seemed truly necessary or particularly helpful. This play requires much less such annotation than other volumes in this series. Indeed, prosodic commentary is distinctly out of place in so free-swinging a farce, which on such matters has caused enormous hand-wringing among scholars. In a word, the prosody in this play is exactly as irregular, even "unreasonable," as is the rowdy farce. In any case, readers should have no problem with the silent "e." Except in the few instances where modern usage syllabifies the "e," whenever an "e" in Shakespeare is *not* silent, it is marked "è". The notation used for prosody, which is also used in the explanation of Elizabethan pronunciation, follows the extremely simple form of my *From Stress to Stress: An Autobiography of English Prosody* (see "Further Reading," near the end of this book). Syllables with metrical stress are capitalized; all other syllables are in lower case letters. I have managed to employ normalized Elizabethan spellings, in most indications of pronunciation, but I have sometimes been obliged to deviate, in the higher interest of being understood.

I have annotated, as well, a limited number of such other matters, sometimes of interpretation, sometimes of general or historical relevance, as have seemed to me seriously worthy of inclusion. These annotations have been most carefully restricted: this is not intended to be a book of literary commentary. It is for that reason that the glossing of metaphors has been severely restricted. There is almost literally no end to discussion and/or analysis of metaphor, especially in Shakespeare. To yield to temptation might well be to double or triple the size of this book—and would also change it from a historically oriented language guide to a work of an unsteadily mixed nature. In the process, I believe, neither language nor literature would be well or clearly served.

Where it seemed useful, and not obstructive of important textual matters, I have modernized spelling, including capitalization. Spelling is not on the whole a basic issue, but Elizabethan punctuation and lineation must be given high respect. The Folio uses few exclamation marks or semicolons, which is to be sure a matter of the conventions of a very different era. Still, our modern preferences cannot be lightly substituted for what is, after a fashion, the closest thing to a Shakespeare manuscript we are likely ever to have. We do not know whether these particular seventeenth-century printers, like most of that time, were responsible for question marks, commas, periods, and, especially, all-purpose colons, or whether these particular printers tried to follow their handwritten sources. Nor do we know if those sources, or what part thereof, might have been in Shakespeare's own hand, But in spite of these equivocations and uncertainties, it remains true that, to a very considerable extent, punctuation tends to result from just how the mind responsible for that punctuating *hears* the text. And twenty-first-century minds have no business, in such matters, overruling seventeenth-century ones. Whoever the compositors were, they were more or less Shakespeare's contemporaries, and we are not.

Accordingly, when the original printed text uses a comma, we are being signaled that *they* (whoever "they" were) heard the text, not coming to a syntactic stop, but continuing to some later stopping point. To replace Folio commas with editorial periods is thus risky and on the whole an undesirable practice. When the Folio text has a colon, what we are being signaled is that *they* heard a syntactic stop—though not necessarily or even usually the particular kind of syntactic stop we associate, today, with the colon. It is therefore inappropriate to substitute editorial commas for Folio colons. It is also inappropriate to employ editorial colons when *their* syntactic usage of colons does not match ours. In general, the closest thing to *their* syntactic sense of the colon is our (and their) period.

The Folio's interrogation (question) marks, too, merit extremely respectful handling, in a play like *Shrew*. In particular, editorial exclamation marks should very rarely be substituted for the Folio's interrogation marks.

It follows from these considerations that the movement and sometimes the meaning of what we must take to be Shakespeare's *Shrew* will at times be different, depending on whose punctuation we follow, *theirs* or our own. I have tried, here, to use the printed seventeenth-century text as a guide to both *hearing* and *understanding* what Shakespeare wrote.

Since the original printed texts of (there not being, as there never are for Shakespeare, any surviving manuscripts) are frequently careless as well as self-contradictory, I have been relatively free with the wording of stage directions—and in some cases have added brief directions, to indicate who is speaking to whom. I have made no emendations; I have necessarily been obliged to make choices. Textual decisions have been annotated when the differences between or among the original printed texts seem either marked or of unusual interest.

In the interests of compactness and brevity, I have employed in my annotations (as consistently as I am able) a number of stylistic and typographical devices:

- The annotation of a single word does not repeat that word

- The annotation of more than one word repeats the words being annotated, which are followed by an equals sign and then by the annotation; the footnote number in the text is placed after the last of the words being annotated

- In annotations of a single word, alternative meanings are usually separated by commas; if there are distinctly different ranges of meaning, the annotations are separated by arabic numerals inside parentheses—(1), (2), and so on; in more complexly worded annotations, alternative meanings expressed by a single word are linked by a forward slash, or solidus: /

- Explanations of textual meaning are not in parentheses; comments about textual meaning are

- Except for proper nouns, the word at the beginning of all annotations is in lower case

- Uncertainties are followed by a question mark, set in parentheses: (?)

- When particularly relevant, "translations" into twenty-first-century English have been added, in parentheses

- Annotations of repeated words are *not* repeated. Explanations of the *first* instance of such common words are followed by the sign ★. Readers may easily track down the first annotation, using the brief Finding List at the back of the book. Words with entirely separate meanings are annotated *only* for meanings no longer current in Modern English.

The most important typographical device here employed is the sign ★ placed after the first (and only) annotation of words and phrases occurring more than once. There is an alphabetically arranged listing of such words and phrases in the Finding List at the back of the book. The Finding List contains no annotations but simply gives the words or phrases themselves and the numbers of the relevant act, the scene within that act, and the footnote number within that scene for the word's first occurrence.

INTRODUCTION

&

S hakespeare's *The Taming of the Shrew* was probably written in 1593–1594, just before Shakespeare turned thirty. It was not published until the Folio edition of 1623. What allows us to assign the play a more-or-less definite date is not this late publication, coming as it does some thirty years after the play's debut, but the 1594 Quarto edition of *The Taming of a* [not "the"] *Shrew,* an anonymous and rather crude derivative, loosely based on what had been heard in the theater. This was what we today call a "rip-off," a commercially motivated project designed to capitalize on Shakespeare's by-then highly successful play. As H. J. Oliver notes, the derivative is "clearly inferior."[1] I believe that even a brief comparison of the opening lines of *Shrew* with the beginning of the derivative makes it clear that Shakespeare neither had nor could have had any hand in its composition. Here, first, is the opening of Shakespeare's *Shrew:*

Sly   I'll pheeze you, in faith.
Hostess A pair of stocks, you rogue!
Sly   Y'are a baggage, the Slys are no rogues. Look in the
        Chronicles, we came in with Richard Conqueror. Therefore,
        paucas pallabris, let the world slide. Sessa!

Hostess You will not pay for the glasses you have burst?

Sly No, not a denier. Go by, Saint Jeronimy, go to thy cold
bed and warm thee.

Hostess I know my remedy; I must go fetch the third-borough.

EXIT HOSTESS

Sly Third, or fourth, or fifth borough, I'll answer him by law.
I'll not budge an inch, boy. Let him come, and kindly.

(Intro.1.1–12)

And Sly immediately falls into a drunken sleep, lying unconscious
on the ground.

Sly's outburst is exactly what we might expect from a hard-
ened drunk. His language is coarse, his logic incoherent. The tav-
ern hostess, assuredly wearily accustomed to such performances,
is laconic and briskly to the point. We do not know, as yet, where
Shakespeare's "Introduction" will take us. But Sly's behavior is
brisk, too, in its alcoholic way. And we are aware, perhaps not entirely consciously, that this is highly professional comic writing,
without wasted words.

Here, in almost total contrast, is the opening of the derivative:

ENTER A TAPSTER, BEATING OUT OF HIS DOORS
SLIE DRUNKEN

Tapster You whoreson drunken slave, you had best be gone,
And empty your drunken paunch somewhere else,
For in this house you shalt not rest tonight.

EXIT TAPSTER

Slie Tilly vally, by crisee, Tapster, I'll feeze you anon.
Fill's 'tother pot, and all's paid for, look you,

I do drink it of mine own instigation. *Omna Bene.*
Here I'll lie a while. Why, Tapster, I say,
Fills a fresh cushion here.
Heigh ho, here's good warm lying.

HE FALLS ASLEEP

Shakespeare's play has been clearly recollected, but only in rough outline. The single verbatim echo, here, is the word "feeze" ("pheeze"). But close examination of all the echoes, here and throughout, makes it clear, as H. J. Oliver notes, "that the 'author' of [the derivative often] is trying to recall phrases he does not even understand."[2] The dialogue is rhetorically inflated, and its pacing is clumsy; the characterizations are frankly nonexistent. Rather than crisp professional comedy, we seem to have been introduced to stock burlesque melodrama.

It is important both to raise and, at least briefly, to deal with these matters. Our understanding of *Shrew,* as a play from Shakespeare's pen, inevitably depends to a considerable extent on our evaluation of the derivative. Shakespeare's Introduction, as Henry Morley wrote in 1856, after watching a revival, "insensibly fades into the play."[3] Considering only the significance of this Introduction (in which Sly's role is extremely important, but entirely—in a word—introductory), we can readily see that in the derivative Sly has a major structural role. He keeps reappearing, playing a large and active role in a very much busier plot, far more rambunctious than that of *Shrew.* The revival Morley witnessed, indeed, was in fact part of a return to the Shakespearean text, which from about 1660 to the end of the eighteenth century had been displaced by a series of adaptations, most of them—significantly—inspired not by Shakespeare's play but by the derivative.

These adaptations belong to literary history, and have no relevance in an edition of this sort.

But their echo can be found in the assertion, still favored by many scholars, that the derivative is "more complete (and therefore more complex and sophisticated) than the Folio text of *The Shrew* . . . [because in it] the Slie-narrative is not a prologue but an extended dramatic framework."[4] And this is neither a lesser nor a trivial matter. The 1623 Folio plainly makes no formal separation. The Introduction is not separately labeled, and in the Folio is indeed presented to us as scenes 1 and 2 of the first act. And what has been conventionally labeled scene 1 is thus, in the Folio, labeled scene 3.[5]

But if the "Introduction" is dramatically disconnected from the play proper, it becomes a display of mere stagecraft, an isolated bit of frolicsome theater that, in the only text we have of the play, can perhaps seem to be more an embarrassment than an adornment. There has been speculation that the "missing" additional parts of the Introduction were in fact performed, in Shakespeare's lifetime, and that, if not written down, they were meant to be performed, *ad libitum,* by the trusted members of Shakespeare's acting company. There is no evidence whatsoever for any part of this.

And now we come to the point. *Shrew* has been understood (*mis*understood) to be a stark, savage, brutal attack on the rights of women. This has over the years troubled a good many critics, though the play has remained continuously popular. "The apparently incomplete nature of the text and the uncertain status of " the derivative cannot tell the whole story, writes Ann Thompson. "A more likely explanation is that literary critics have concurred in the opinion . . . that the play is 'disgusting' and 'barbaric.'"[6]

And yet it has also been said that the idea of male superiority is "a doctrine which Shakespeare must have adopted in cold blood, for on the evidence of the other plays it was not his own."[7]

Indeed, women are in fact not only portrayed favorably, in all of Shakespeare (and most especially in the comedies), but are almost invariably shown to be smarter and more capable than men. Portia, in *The Merchant of Venice,* is in this regard prototypical. Confined and retiring as she is said to be, not only is she demonstrably the "better half" of her forthcoming marriage, but (dressed in male clothing) she is capable (with to be sure significant professional assistance) of performing brilliantly as a lawyer, though as a mere female she has no background or training in the legal arts.

However, the Introduction is *not* separate from the play proper. Like all the relatively few prologues to Shakespeare's plays, it has been designed to announce the subject matter, the perspective, the tone, and even the end result of the play that follows. Shakespeare has elsewhere demonstrated that he is capable of accomplishing this in no more than the 14 lines of a sonnet (as he does in *Romeo and Juliet*). And except for the Introduction to *Shrew,* Shakespeare's "Prologues" and preparatory "Choruses" invariably run to no more than 30 or 40 lines. Shakespeare's "Epilogues" are, without exception, no more than about half that length. Here, however, without counting Sly's pro forma 5-line reappearance, later in the first act, *Shrew*'s Introduction runs to an impressive total of 274 lines. The intensely dramatic 155-line first scene in *Hamlet* is barely half this long; the first scene of *Othello* runs to 185 lines; and even the singularly extensive first scene of *King Lear* is only twenty or thirty lines longer, depending on whether we measure the Quarto or the Folio text of that play. Accordingly, introductory material that has roughly 900 percent the heft of all similar introductory material is not only unique but requires that we attempt to understand what, in this Introduction and no place else in his work, Shakespeare is up to.

"The relationship between Petruchio and Katherina is obviously the heart of the problem; . . . critics have always found it difficult to decide how seriously we should view these particular characters."[8] It is useful to remind ourselves, first, that "Petruchio is [the] hero of a farce, not of a romance."[9] More accurately, perhaps, Petruchio is the primary *male* figure in a farce.

> [We should view comic] scenes as far as possible in the light of the common experiences of sixteenth-century spectators; for one would assume that an author's attempt to produce laughter would proceed along the lines of whatever were the age's comic expectations and proclivities. . . . When in more sophisticated circumstances Ben Jonson and his friends established rules for their meeting in the Apollo chamber of the Old Devil Tavern, they seem to have had in mind . . . the [time's] immoderate joy. . . . [I]t should not be surprising that Shakespeare and his contemporaries showed a red-bloodedness that did not exclude mental dexterity but that also utilized the laughter and merriment of the "vulgar." . . . Elizabethan living, however magnificent, [was always] close to the "crude." . . . [And] when one turns to a more detailed consideration of Elizabethan merriment, . . . a logical beginning would be to examine some aspects of comic wooing. No motif was more widespread. . . . Parodies of wooing and marriage usually emphasized shrewish wives

and the noisy bawdry of brawling females. . . . Ballads
constantly celebrated the shrew.[10]

The subject matter employed for *Shrew*'s farce is without a doubt
the endless, timeless discussion as to which sex outperforms/out-
weighs the other. But the function of *Shrew*'s Introduction is
twofold. First, to make us aware that the play is, also without a
doubt, farcical, not in any way a serious presentation, and second,
to begin introducing the sort of dramatic personages who are to
be made fun of. In Shakespeare's Introduction, plainly, the targets
are on one hand a drunken, beggared tinker (male), and on the
other an arrogant, smugly aristocratic lord (male), whose pillory-
ing of the tinker is more than casually reminiscent of the satirical
portrait of the Duke and Duchess, in the second part of another
and roughly contemporary work, Miguel de Cervantes's *Don
Quijote*. The Duke and Duchess are aristocrats who maltreat for
their private amusement anyone and everyone below their lordly
stations.

Is Shakespeare's Introduction meant to signal anything more
than that what follows is typical farce? I do not think Shakespeare
would have wasted his time and energy, and certainly not to this
comparatively large exent, if there had not been more involved.
We need to move forward, to the opening of the play proper,
scene 1. When the Introduction fades insensibly into this larger
spectacle, the setting switches from rural England to Padua. And
Shakespeare craftily pretends, at first, to be taking us in a new and
different direction. But the first of the "Italian" characters, like
those of the "English" sort, are male. And these new characters,
Lucentio and Tranio, are presented to us by way of forty-seven
placid, conventional lines, deliberately (but, as we soon learn,

mockingly) steeped in classical learning and utterly typical Humanist morality.

> Here let us breathe, and haply institute
> A course of learning and ingenious studies.
> . . . .
> And therefore Tranio, for the time I study,
> Virtue and that part of philosophy
> Will I apply, that treats of happiness,
> By virtue specially to be achieved. (1.1.8–9, 17–20)

And after this, as quick as quicksilver, the fun begins once more and we return to the farce that we have most emphatically been led to expect. The setting is indeed different; the characters are apparently also different. But the *tone* is absolutely the same. Kate et al. burst into our view and the learned, platitudinous "Humanists" literally step to the side of the stage. And indeed, by the time they return to stage center, these "wise philosophers" have been utterly transformed. Their platitudes evaporate into the nothingness from which they emerged, vividly exposed as mere posturing—and, once again, as explicitly male posturing. In the rest of the play, nothing is studied, much less the philosophy of virtue.

In just under a hundred lines, scene 1 then rapidly introduces us to the main figures of the play proper: (1) the harried father, Baptista; (2) the comical old pantaloon, Gremio, a stock character (whose very name helps prepare us for another stock figure of comedy, Grumio, Petruchio's disrespectful, wise-cracking servant); (3) the thoroughly bad-tempered older sister, Kate; (4) the utterly sweet (blatantly, unbelievably sweet) younger sister, Bianca; and (5) the lovelorn suitor for Bianca's hand, Hortensio. Lucentio, so briefly a classics-quoting Humanist, has suddenly (after the time-honored way of farces) become yet another of the many lovelorn Bianca-worshippers: "I burn, I pine, I perish," he declares (1.1.152). And the farcical servant, Tranio, like so many other "good" servants tirelessly helpful, has settled into what will be his role for the balance of the play, namely, the dutiful effectuator of his master's desires.

Once Sly has been very briefly returned, and disposed of, Shakespeare immediately introduces Kate's future husband, Petruchio. And, having just finished reminding us of the farcical joke that has been played on Christopher Sly (and thereby having completely exhausted the need for Christopher Sly), Shakespeare does not dally before restarting the full-bore engines of the farce. Petruchio is given exactly four calm, placid lines. In the fifth, he breaks into full farcical flight:

Petruchio Verona, for a while I take my leave
　　To see my friends in Padua, but of all
　　My best belovèd and approvèd friend,
　　Hortensio, and I trow this is his house.
　　Here, sirrah Grumio, knock, I say. (1.2.1–5)

The Elizabethan audience would have recognized at once, hearing Petruchio's fifth line, that they were to be treated to a ludicrously defective male-on-male master-servant relationship. Grumio as a farcical figure will plainly have, in good part, the role of "bad servant," patently troublesome, balky, and—worst of all—blazingly independent.[11] Grumio's response to his master's directive—"knock, I say"—is insolent, witty, and fractious: "Knock, sir? Whom should I knock? Is there any man who has rebused your worship?" (1.2.9–10). Servant and master thereafter progress rapidly, in a mere twelve lines, through uproarious, burlesque-quality repartee to outright physical violence. Both men are patently, and very deliberately, made ridiculous.

Are we to take this, as so many critics take Petruchio's interaction with Kate, for an exposition of Shakespeare's closely held, intimate views on masters and servants? Hardly. Exactly as Kate's initially shrewish behavior stems from the pure, standard farce of the time (as many, many critics have more than fully demonstrated), so too standard farce is the origin of Petruchio and Grumio's tumbling idiocy. More: the Petruchio to whom we are now introduced is, for better or worse, all the Petruchio we are ever going to see and, by necessary extension, all the Petruchio there is meant to be. Shakespeare has thus irrevocably established clown-Petruchio—a wonderfully drawn stage figure, vastly loud and energetic, outlandish, bold, utterly single-minded and determinedly two-dimensional. Like the clownish figure he is meant to be, he never changes or develops. Writing this carefully constructed farce, Shakespeare cannot permit a character so basic to his farce to get out of hand and pretend to be taken as seriously as Hamlet or Othello. Or, in fact, to be taken seriously at all. An Abbott and Costello farce is an Abbott and Costello farce. Period. It is no reflection on the quality of a farce to insist on its farcicality.

Neither is there either development or change in the play's other characterizations. *Shrew* is strictly, as per the dictionary definition of "farce," an "artificial presentation," full of "ridiculous confusions." Kate may *seem* to change. But other than those who see *Shrew* as a record of serious abuse, even brutality, ending with a hopeless, defenseless surrender by a broken young woman,[12] not many people have ever been persuaded that Kate's incredible final speech is, in fact, anything but incredible—for what else would or could it be, as the conclusion to a riotous farce? Kate is not Lear, forced to deal with vast eruptions of change, profoundly altering the nature of his world. She is a farcical shrew, no more, no less. Can we imagine a truly determined shrew running off weeping, in act 3, scene 2, when her intended (though perhaps – it is not at all clear that in fact he is—unwelcome) has not appeared in time? "*The Taming of the Shrew* participates in a tenacious popular tradition of depicting domestic violence as funny. . . . In all the texts about shrews and shrew taming here, the women instigate the violence or conflict and thus seem to provoke retaliation. Furthermore, the husband's . . . punishments are depicted as a last resort; they are not angry and uncontrolled actions, but rather a conscious strategy for governing the unruly."[13] For an Elizabethan audience, more than familiar with the stock shrews of the time, to affix the label of "shrew" to a woman was more than sufficient to fully and satisfyingly place her. The audience would have howled with delight as Kate gets her long overdue comeuppance. Oliver, who describes *Shrew* as a "none-too-serious comedy," observes that "the very costume worn by the boy playing Katherine may have identified her as nothing but a shrew: in short, there may have been as much likelihood of the audience's sympathizing with Katherine . . . as there is of a twentieth-century music-hall audience's feeling sorry for a mother-in-law. The very first words addressed to Kate also take it for granted that she has no humanity: Gremio's reply to Baptista's invitation to court his elder daughter is 'To cart her rather. She's too rough for me'— which virtually calls Kate to her face a prostitute."[14]

Shrews and their "noble conquerors"—can Petruchio be seen as noble?—are thus rolled through the farcical hoops. Neither male nor female dominance, and neither male superiority nor female, is being examined, much less celebrated. To argue that the satirical impetus of farce is equivalent to an ideological polemic amounts, in short, to a serious error in perception. Whether we ourselves happen to be male or female, we can and should laugh (as we are meant to) at both Petruchio and Kate without the slightest concern about compromising our gendered condition or status.

For there are better and potentially more interesting suppositions, linked not to the totally problematic 1594 derivative but founded in the text of *Shrew*. Arguably, these suppositions can help us account for some aspects of Shakespeare's Introduction and of the rollicking farce that follows it. As it happens, the Introduction is set not in some abstract England but in rural Warwickshire, which contains not only Warwick itself, and the Forest of Arden, but also Stratford on Avon. It is, in a word, Shakespeare's home ground. "The whole atmosphere of rural Warwickshire," says Thompson, "with its hunting lords, drunken tinkers and fat alewives is clearly drawn (perhaps somewhat rosily) from his own youthful experience."[15] The Introduction's main figure, Christopher Sly, takes his very name from Warwickshire. The fact that "The name 'Sly' has been found in both Warwickshire and London records" indicates, as to the name's presence in London, no more than predictable migration from the provinces into the great city of London.[16]

> Am I not Christopher Sly, old Sly's son of Burton-heath, by birth a peddler, by education a cardmaker, by transmutation a bearherd, and now by present profession a tinker? Ask Marian Hackett, the fat ale-wife of Wincot, if she know me not. (Intro.2.15–20)

Burton-heath is Barton-on-the-Heath, which is south of Stratford; Rowse informs us that "Shakespeare's uncle and aunt, the Lamberts, lived" there.[17] Wincot is either a village near Stratford, or "possibly Wilmcote, where Shakespeare's mother came from," says Rowse (though Oliver rejects this possibility), adding that "There were Hackets around Stratford, as we know from the parish registers . . .").[18] The jesting Lord's first servingman informs Sly that, when in his fifteen-year-long sleep,

> . . . though you lay here in this goodly chamber,
> Yet would you say ye were beaten out of door,
> And rail upon the hostess of the house,
> And say you would present her at the leet [i.e., manor court]
> Because she brought stone jugs and no sealed quarts.
> Sometimes you would call out for Cicely Hacket
> (Intro.2.81–86)

The hostess being Marian Hacket, as Sly himself has told us, Cicely is likely to have been her daughter and helper. The Lord's third servingman helpfully refers to "Stephen Sly and old John Naps of Greece, / And Peter Turph and Henry Pimpernell, / And twenty more such names and men as these" (1.2.90–92). Rowse explains that "Greece" is a misprint for Greet, "not far away" from Stratford. It makes good Warwickshire sense, too, that Sly claims to have been a "cardmaker"—that is, one involved in the making of "iron-toothed instruments for combing wool . . . , a likely trade for one dwelling on the edge of the Cotswolds [southwest of Stratford], famous in Shakespeare's day for producing sheep and wool."[19]

It is not known whether John Naps, Peter Turph, and Henry Pimpernell are the names of actual Warwickshire residents. Heilman, among others, suspects that they may well be.[20] And why not? If in fact *Shrew* was not a stage production retrospective of Shakespeare's Warwickshire youth, but celebratory of a current and perhaps substantial Warwickshire presence in a flesh-and-blood theater audience, would Shakespeare have referred to Warwickshire folk *except* by their real names? There appears to be far too much of Warwickshire in his Introduction, too many small, wonderfully concrete details, too many then highly recognizable names, too jolly a well-located farce, for the evocation of place and manners to have been merely nostalgic. Rural playgoers, themselves inclined to be somewhat socially retrogressive, would surely have taken special delight in Kate's final speech. It might well have been exactly what such playgoers would most want to hear from the likes of Kate. There may even be a buried clue in the second player's still mysterious reference to "Soto":

Lord   This fellow I remember
    Since once he played a farmer's eldest son. –
    'Twas where you wooed the gentlewoman so well.
    I have forgot your name; but sure that part
    Was aptly fitted and naturally performed.
Second Player I think 'twas Soto that your honor means.
Lord   'Tis very true; thou didst it excellent.
    (Intro. 1.80–86)

The Soto allusion seems too particular to have been fanciful, but it has yet to be deciphered.[21] This might well be a contemporary (again, rather than a retrospective) reference to a traveling player or players, and to a play known equally to Shakespeare and to his Warwickshire friends and acquaintances, though unknown to us. That seems considerably less startling than taking Petruchio and his antics as malicious anti-female polemic.

Enjoy this long-celebrated farce and its energetic characters much as you might, say, enjoy any one of the James Bond movies, without fearing for the lives of any of the many many people "killed" along the way. A farce is a game—and no one plays it better than Shakespeare.

Notes

1. H. J. Oliver, ed., *The Taming of the Shrew* (Oxford: Clarendon Press, 1982), 14.

2. Oliver, *Taming of the Shrew,* 19.

3. Gamini Salgado, *Eyewitnesses of Shakespeare* (New York: Barnes and Noble, 1975), 77.

4. Graham Holderness and Bryan Loughrey, eds., *A Pleasant Conceited Historie, Called The Taming of a Shrew* (New York: Harvest Wheatsheaf, 1992), 16–17.

5. It was Alexander Pope, in his 1723 edition, who first used a separate heading for the play's first two scenes. Virtually all editors, ever since, have followed Pope, not the Folio – though the latter is in every sense closer to Shakespeare. Though I have nominally followed this later editorial practice (although altering the subtitle from Pope's "Induction" to the less restrictive "Introduction"), I have done so only for ease of cross-reference to three hundred years of literary citation.

6. Ann Thompson, ed., *The Taming of the Shrew* (Cambridge: Cambridge University Press, 1984), 25.

7. Mark Van Doren, *Shakespeare* (New York: Holt, 1939), 37.

8. Thompson, *Taming of the Shrew,* 25.

9. Van Doren, *Shakespeare,* 37.

10. Ernest William Talbert, *Elizabethan Drama and Shakespeare's Early Plays* (New York: Gordian, 1973), 8, 11, 13, 17.

11. Not all masters were so punctilious as Sir John Harington, who wrote out a solemn code for his servants: "Item, that none toy with the maids, on pain of 4 pence. Item, that none swear any oath, upon pain for every

oath 1 pence." Quoted in A. L. Rowse, *The Elizabethan Renaissance: The Life of the Society* (London: History Book Club, 1971), 111.

12. "One must remember . . . that in Petruchio's farmhouse Kate is deprived of sleep, food, and the protection of family and female companionship—techniques akin to modern methods of torture and brainwashing. . . . This is horrifying, even if the horror is mitigated by the laughter-inducing techniques of knockabout farce." Jean Howard, quoted in Stephen Greenblatt, ed., *The Norton Shakespeare* (New York: Norton, 1997), 139.

13. Frances E. Dolan, ed., *The Taming of the Shrew: Texts and Contexts* (Boston: Bedford, 1996), 245.

14. Oliver, *Taming of the Shrew*, 42, 51. Prostitutes, and other offenders against the laws of the land, were publicly paraded about in carts. Chrétien de Troyes's *Lancelot*, subtitled "The Knight of the Cart," demonstrates the venerability and the power of this shaming ritual.

15. Thompson, *Taming of the Shrew*, 15.

16. Oliver, *Taming of the Shrew*, 89n.

17. A. L. Rowse, *The Annotated Shakespeare*, vol. 1 (New York: Clarkson Potter, 1978), 118.

18. Rowse, 98n.

19. Oliver, *Taming of the Shrew*, 98n.

20. Robert B. Heilman, ed., *The Taming of the Shrew* (New York: Signet, 1966), 54n.

21. Attempts to tie "Soto" to a 1620 play by John Fletcher, *Women Pleased*, have failed both on narrative and chronological grounds—though Heilman conjectures that "Soto" was inserted into Shakespeare's text between 1620 and *Shrew*'s publication in 1623 (*Taming of the Shrew*, 48n).

SOME ESSENTIALS OF THE
SHAKESPEAREAN STAGE

ℬ

The Stage

- There was no *scenery* (backdrops, flats, and so on).

- Compared to today's elaborate, high-tech productions, the Elizabethan stage had few *on-stage* props. These were mostly handheld: a sword or dagger, a torch or candle, a cup or flask. Larger props, such as furniture, were used sparingly.

- Costumes (some of which were upper-class castoffs, belonging to the individual actors) were elaborate. As in most premodern and very hierarchical societies, clothing was the distinctive mark of who and what a person was.

- What the actors *spoke,* accordingly, contained both the dramatic and narrative material we have come to expect in a theater (or movie house) and (1) the setting, including details of the time of day, the weather, and so on, and (2) the occasion. The *dramaturgy* is thus very different from that of our own time, requiring much more attention to verbal and gestural matters. Strict realism was neither intended nor, under the circumstances, possible.

- There was *no curtain*. Actors entered and left via doors in the back of the stage, behind which was the "tiring-room," where actors put on or changed their costumes.

- In *public theaters* (which were open-air structures), there was no *lighting;* performances could take place only in daylight hours.

- For *private* theaters, located in large halls of aristocratic houses, candlelight illumination was possible.

The Actors

- Actors worked in *professional,* for-profit companies, sometimes organized and owned by other actors, and sometimes by entrepreneurs who could afford to erect or rent the company's building. Public theaters could hold, on average, two thousand playgoers, most of whom viewed and listened while standing. Significant profits could be and were made. Private theaters were smaller, more exclusive.

- There was *no director.* A book-holder/prompter/props manager, standing in the tiring-room behind the backstage doors, worked from a text marked with entrances and exits and notations of any special effects required for that particular script. A few such books have survived. Actors had texts only of their own parts, speeches being cued to a few prior words. There were few and often no rehearsals, in our modern use of the term, though there was often some coaching of individuals. Since Shakespeare's England was largely an oral culture, actors learned their parts rapidly and retained them for years. This was *repertory* theater, repeating popular plays and introducing some new ones each season.

- *Women* were not permitted on the professional stage. Most female roles were acted by *boys;* elderly women were played by grown men.

The Audience

- London's professional theater operated in what might be called a "red-light" district, featuring brothels, restaurants, and the kind of *open-air entertainment* then most popular, like bear-baiting (in which a bear, tied to a stake, was set on by dogs).

- A theater audience, like most of the population of Shakespeare's England, was largely made up of *illiterates.* Being able to read and write, however, had nothing to do with intelligence or concern with language, narrative, and characterization. People attracted to the theater tended to be both extremely verbal and extremely volatile. Actors were sometimes attacked, when the audience was dissatisfied; quarrels and fights were relatively common. Women were regularly in attendance, though no reliable statistics exist.

- Drama did not have the cultural esteem it has in our time, and plays were not regularly printed. Shakespeare's often appeared in book form, but not with any supervision or other involvement on his part. He wrote a good deal of nondramatic poetry as well, yet so far as we know he did not authorize or supervise *any* work of his that appeared in print during his lifetime.

- Playgoers, who had paid good money to see and hear, plainly gave dramatic performances careful, detailed attention. For some closer examination of such matters, see Burton Raffel, "Who Heard the Rhymes and How: Shakespeare's Dramaturgical Signals," *Oral Tradition* 11 (October 1996): 190–221, and Raffel, "Metrical Dramaturgy in Shakespeare's Earlier Plays," *CEA Critic* 57 (Spring–Summer 1995): 51–65.

The Taming of the Shrew

ℰℬ

CHARACTERS (DRAMATIS PERSONAE)

Shakespeare's Introduction and final lines of act 1, scene 1

A lord
Christopher Sly (a beggar and a tinker)[1]
Hostess (of an alehouse)
Page[2]
Players[3]
Huntsmen
Servants

Acts 1–5

Petruchio (gentleman of Verona)
Grumio (Petruchio's personal servant)
Curtis, Nathaniel, Philip, Joseph, Nicholas, Peter (Petruchio's servants)
Baptista Minola (rich man of Padua, father of Kate and Bianca)
Vincentio (Lucentio's father)
Lucentio (in love with Bianca)
Tranio (Lucentio's personal servant)
Biondello (Lucentio's servant)
Hortensio (young man in love with Bianca)
Gremio (elderly man in love with Bianca)
Pedant[4]
Tailor
Haberdasher
Servants
Kate (Katherina, older daughter of Baptista)
Bianca (younger daughter of Baptista)
A widow

1 itinerant pot-mender★
2 young male servant
3 actors★
4 schoolmaster★

Shakespeare's Introduction[1]

&

SCENE I

In front of an alehouse

ENTER HOSTESS[2] AND SLY

Sly   I'll pheeze[3] you, in faith.[4]

Hostess   A pair of stocks,[5] you rogue![6]

Sly   Y'are a baggage,[7] the Slys are no rogues. Look in the
Chronicles,[8] we came in with Richard Conqueror.[9]
Therefore, paucas pallabris,[10] let the world slide.[11] Sessa![12]   5

1 untitled in Folio; Alexander Pope's 1723 edition used the title "Induction"
   (a Latinate way of saying "Introduction"), which has been employed ever
   since
2 mistress of an inn/public house
3 smash, take care of
4 in truth, really★
5 punishment device, in which offenders' feet, hands, or both were clamped
   between notched-out boards
6 rascal, beggar, tramp★
7 (1) rubbish, trash, (2) whore
8 historical records
9 William the Conqueror arrived in England in 1066, a fact universally
   known
10 *pocas palabras* (Spanish): fewer words ("shut up")
11 that's enough, let it all go
12 (?) desist, stop ("cease")

Hostess You will not pay for the glasses you have burst?

Sly   No, not a denier.[13] Go by,[14] Saint Jeronimy,[15] go to thy
   cold bed and warm thee.

Hostess I know my remedy, I must go fetch the third-borough.[16]

EXIT HOSTESS

10 *Sly*   Third, or fourth, or fifth borough, I'll answer him[17] by
   law.[18] I'll not budge an inch, boy.[19] Let him come, and
   kindly.[20]

LIES DOWN ON THE GROUND, AND FALLS
INTO A DRUNKEN SLEEP

SOUND OF HUNTING HORNS. ENTER A LORD,
WITH HUNTSMEN AND SERVANTS

Lord   Huntsman, I charge[21] thee, tender well[22] my
   hounds.
   Brach[23] Merriman, the poor cur,[24] is embossed.[25]

---

13 small French copper coin
14 leave, go away
15 In Thomas Kyd's popular and often-quoted play *The Spanish Tragedy,* the
   main character says to himself, "Hieronimo, beware! Go by, go by!"
   (3,12.31)
16 local/petty constable (Old English "frithborh": surety for peace; Middle English "thridboro")
17 answer him = defend myself to him
18 by law = at law, law for law
19 by God, let me tell you
20 gladly, welcome
21 command*
22 tender well = take good care of
23 hound that hunts by scent (noun; some editors interpret "brach" as a verb:
   medicate/let breathe)
24 dog (without negative connotation)
25 exhausted, foaming at the mouth

And couple[26] Clowder[27] with the deep-mouthed brach.[28]   15

Saw'st thou not, boy,[29] how Silver made it good[30]

At the hedge-corner,[31] in the coldest fault?[32]

I would not lose the dog for twenty pound.

Huntsman 1 Why, Bellman is as good as he, my lord,

He cried upon it[33] at the merest loss,[34]   20

And twice today picked out the dullest[35] scent.

Trust me, I take him for the better dog.

Lord   Thou art a fool. If Echo were as fleet,[36]

I would esteem[37] him worth a dozen such.

But sup[38] them well, and look unto[39] them all.   25

Tomorrow I intend to hunt again.

Huntsman 1 I will, my lord.

Lord   (*seeing Sly*) What's here? One dead, or drunk? See

doth he breathe.[40]

Huntsman 2 He breathes, my lord. Were he not warmed with ale,

This were[41] a bed but[42] cold to sleep so soundly.   30

26 mate
27 (?) noisemaker
28 deep-mouthed brach = sonorous-voiced bitch
29 lad, young man
30 made it good = compensated for the cold/lost scent
31 boundary bushes
32 coldest fault = totally vanished scent
33 cried upon it = called/gave tongue
34 merest loss = most complete absence of scent
35 weakest
36 swift
37 value
38 feed
39 look unto = take care of*
40 see doth he breathe = see if he's breathing
41 would be (subjunctive)
42 only, very, really

Lord	O monstrous[43] beast,[44] how like a swine he lies!
	Grim death, how foul and loathsome is thine image.[45]
	Sirs,[46] I will practice[47] on this drunken man.
	What think you, if he were conveyed to bed,[48]

35 Wrapped in sweet[49] clothes, rings[50] put upon his fingers,

A most delicious banquet[51] by his bed,

And brave[52] attendants near him when he wakes,

Would not the beggar then forget himself?[53]

Huntsman 1 Believe me, lord, I think he cannot choose.[54]

40 *Huntsman 2* It would seem strange unto him when he waked.

Lord Even as[55] a flattering dream or worthless fancy.[56]

Then take[57] him up, and manage[58] well the jest.

Carry him gently[59] to my fairest chamber,[60]

And hang it round[61] with all my wanton[62] pictures.

---

43 unnatural, abnormal
44 the animal nature in man★ (man and beast as opposites)
45 likeness, portrait
46 gentlemen (condescending, since they are obviously not gentlemen, i.e., high-/well-born)
47 play tricks
48 conveyed to bed = carried/brought to bed (a "bed" was then expensive, four-posted, curtained, and unfamiliar to Sly)
49 pleasant-smelling,★ clean
50 (precious metal, and jeweled; not worn by beggars)
51 delicious banquet = delightful/pleasing small/casual meal (often dessert-like)★
52 finely dressed/uniformed
53 who he is (social status)
54 cannot choose = will have no choice, must
55 even as = exactly like★
56 hallucination, fantasy (something imagined)
57 raise, pick, lift
58 conduct, perform
59 softly, carefully
60 fairest chamber = best-looking/most handsome/beautiful★ room
61 hang it round = hang all around it
62 gay ("brightly colored")

Balm[63] his foul[64] head in warm distillèd waters,[65]   45
And burn sweet[66] wood to make the lodging[67] sweet.
Procure me[68] music ready when he wakes,
To make a dulcet[69] and a heavenly sound.
And if he chance[70] to speak, be ready straight,[71]
And with a low submissive reverence[72]   50
Say, "What is it your honor will command?"[73]
Let one[74] attend him with a silver basin
Full of rose-water,[75] and bestrewed[76] with flowers,
Another bear the ewer,[77] the third a diaper,[78]
And say, "Will't please your lordship cool[79] your hands?"   55
Some one be ready with a costly[80] suit,
And ask him what apparel he will wear.
Another tell him of his hounds and horse,
And that his lady mourns at his disease.
Persuade him that he hath been lunatic,   60

63 anoint
64 dirty, muddy★ (the word was widely used for negatives physical,
   psychological, and moral)
65 distillèd waters = purified and perfumed liquids / decoctions
66 fragrant
67 room
68 procure me = arrange on my behalf / for me
69 agreeable, pleasant, sweet
70 happens★
71 at once, immediately★
72 bow, show of respect
73 will command = wishes to order / demand
74 someone
75 water perfumed with the fragrance of roses
76 covered over / scattered
77 water jug with a wide spout★
78 towel
79 refresh
80 lavish, sumptuous

And when[81] he says he is, say that he dreams,

For he is nothing but a mighty[82] lord.

This do, and do[83] it kindly, gentle[84] sirs,

It will be pastime passing excellent,[85]

65　If it be husbanded[86] with modesty.[87]

Huntsman 1　My lord, I warrant[88] you we will play our part

As[89] he shall think by our true diligence[90]

He is no less than what we say he is.

Lord　　　　Take him up gently, and to bed with him,

70　And each one to his office[91] when he wakes.

SLY IS CARRIED OUT

TRUMPET SOUNDS[92]

Sirrah,[93] go see what trumpet 'tis that sounds

EXIT SERVANT

Belike[94] some noble gentleman[95] that means,

---

81 if
82 wealthy, highborn★
83 if you do
84 well-born, gentlemanly
85 pastime passing excellent = surpassingly / exceedingly★ good sport / amusement
86 managed
87 moderation, self-control
88 promise, guarantee★
89 so that
90 true diligence = faithful / real★ earnest efforts
91 duty, service ("job")★
92 blows (verb)
93 term of address used with inferiors and children★
94 probably★
95 noble gentleman = illustrious / high-ranking man of good birth / breeding★

Traveling some journey, to repose[96] him here.

SERVANT RETURNS

How now?[97] Who is it?

Servant   An[98] it please your honor,[99] players

That offer service[100] to your lordship.   75

Lord   Bid[101] them come near.[102]

ENTER PLAYERS

                    Now fellows,[103] you are

welcome.

Players   We thank your honor.

Lord   Do you intend to stay[104] with me tonight?

Player   So[105] please your lordship to accept our duty.[106]

Lor.   With all my heart. This fellow I remember,   80

Since once[107] he played a farmer's eldest son —

'Twas where you wooed the gentlewoman[108] so well.

I have forgot your name. But sure[109] that part

96 spend the night (there were no hotels; inns were too public for noble
     gentlemen, and courtesy was readily extended from one aristocrat to
     another)
97 in modern usage, "what's going on?"★
98 if★
99 person deserving respect, usually for rank or title
100 work for hire★
101 invite, tell
102 come near = approach
103 men (familiar form of address)★
104 lodge
105 if it
106 deference, respect, service, work★
107 since once = from when
108 woman of good birth/breeding
109 certainly

Was aptly fitted[110] and naturally[111] performed.

85   *Player*   I think 'twas Soto that your honor means.

  Lord   'Tis very true,[112] thou didst it excellent.

    Well, you are[113] come to me in happy[114] time,

    The rather for[115] I have some sport[116] in hand

    Wherein your cunning[117] can assist me much.

90   There is a lord will hear you play[118] tonight,

    But I am doubtful of your modesties,[119]

    Lest – over-eying of[120] his odd behavior,

    For yet[121] his honor never heard a play –

    You break[122] into some merry passion[123]

95   And so[124] offend him. For I tell you sirs,

    If you should smile, he grows impatient.[125]

  Player   Fear not my lord, we can contain ourselves,

    Were he[126] the veriest antic[127] in the world.

  Lord   Go sirrah, take them to the buttery,[128]

---

110 aptly fitted = appropriate for/well-suited to you
111 realistically
112 very true = completely/absolutely right
113 have
114 in happy = at a favorable/fortunate
115 the rather for = the more so because
116 amusement, entertainment, diversion★
117 craft, skill★
118 perform, act
119 self-control
120 over-eying of = observing
121 as yet, until now
122 burst
123 fit, emotion
124 thus
125 irritable, annoyed★
126 were he = even if he were
127 clown
128 pantry, storeroom for food and drink

And give them friendly welcome every one,   100
Let them want[129] nothing that my house affords.[130]

EXIT SERVANT WITH PLAYERS

Sirrah, go you to Bartholomew my page,
And see him[131] dressed in all suits like[132] a lady.[133]
That done, conduct[134] him to the drunkard's chamber,
And call him Madam, do him obeisance.[135]   105
Tell him from me, as he will win my love,[136]
He bear[137] himself with honorable action,[138]
Such as he hath observed in noble ladies
Unto their lords,[139] by them accomplishèd.[140]
Such duty to the drunkard let him do,   110
With soft low tongue and lowly[141] courtesy,
And say "What is't your honor will command,
Wherein your lady[142] and your humble[143] wife
May show her duty, and make known her love?"
And then with kind[144] embracements, tempting kisses,   115

129 lack★ (verb)
130 can give/supply
131 see him = see to it that he is
132 all suits like = completely in the clothing of
133 gentlewoman
134 escort, bring
135 do him obeisance = pay him respect
136 regard, favor
137 is to bear
138 honorable action = decent/respectful behavior★
139 husbands
140 performed
141 humble, submissive (positive sense)★
142 lady love ("object of chivalric devotion")
143 lowly (positive sense)
144 proper, natural★

And with declining head into his bosom[145]
Bid him[146] shed tears, as being overjoyed
To see her noble lord restored to health,
Who for this seven years hath esteemed him[147]
120   No better than a poor and loathsome beggar.
And if the boy have not a woman's gift
To rain a shower of commanded[148] tears,
An onion will do well for such a shift,[149]
Which in a napkin, being close conveyed,[150]
125   Shall in despite[151] enforce a watery eye.
See this dispatched[152] with all the haste thou canst,
Anon[153] I'll give thee more instructions.

EXIT SERVANT

I know the boy will well usurp[154] the grace,[155]
Voice, gait,[156] and action of a gentlewoman.
130   I long to hear him call the drunkard "husband,"
And how my men will stay[157] themselves from laughter,

---

145 declining head into his bosom = (1) "her" head bent to Sly's chest, or
   (2) lying against Sly's chest, with "her" head lowered/bent downward
146 "her" (the page)
147 esteemed him = thought himself
148 forced
149 joke, device
150 close conveyed = hidden (conveyed = carried: not linguistically necessary
   in modern usage)
151 in despite = notwithstanding, in spite of himself ★
152 done, accomplished
153 immediately, in a very short time
154 assume, borrow, employ
155 gracefulness
156 manner of walking/moving ★
157 stop

When they do homage to this simple peasant.[158]
I'll in[159] to counsel[160] them. Haply[161] my presence
May well[162] abate[163] the over-merry spleen,[164]
Which otherwise would grow[165] into extremes.   135

EXEUNT

158 simple peasant = humble/foolish★ clod/clown
159 go in
160 advise★
161 perhaps, maybe★
162 usefully, rightly
163 do away with, curtail, lower
164 the spleen was thought to be the source of laughter
165 get to be, become

SCENE 2

Bedroom in the Lord's house[1]

SLY IN A RICH NIGHTSHIRT, WITH SERVANTS,
SOME WITH APPAREL, BASIN, EWER, ETC., AND LORD[2]

Sly   For God's sake, a pot[3] of small ale.[4]

Servant 1 Will't please your lordship drink a cup[5] of sack?[6]

Servant 2 Will't please your honor taste of[7] these conserves?[8]

Servant 3 What raiment[9] will your honor wear today?

5 *Sly*   I am Christophero Sly, call not me "honor" nor
          "lordship." I ne'er drank sack in my life. And if you give me
          any conserves, give me conserves of beef.[10] Ne'er ask me
          what raiment I'll wear, for I have no more doublets[11] than
          backs, no more stockings than legs, nor no more shoes than
10   feet – nay, sometime more feet than shoes, or such shoes as
          my toes look through the over-leather.[12]

Lord   Heaven cease[13] this idle humor[14] in your honor!
          O that a mighty man of such descent,

1 the scene is set on a raised part of the stage, either the balcony (as in *Romeo and Juliet*) or perhaps a platform: the Folio, our only text for the play, sets this scene "aloft")
2 dressed like a servant
3 container, metal or pottery, used to hold liquid
4 of low alcohol content/inferior
5 wine cup
6 imported white wine, from Spain and the Canary Isles
7 taste of = taste
8 confections, preserves (fruit and sugar)
9 clothing★
10 conserves of beef = preserved/dried/pickled beef
11 jacket-like undercoat, close-fitting★
12 upper leather
13 heaven cease = may heaven stop
14 idle humor = foolish/silly/useless mood/disposition★

Of such possessions, and so[15] high esteem,[16]
Should be infused[17] with so foul a spirit![18]   15

Sly   What, would you[19] make me mad?[20] Am not I
Christopher Sly, old Sly's son of Burton-heath,[21] by birth a
peddler,[22] by education a card-maker,[23] by transmutation[24]
a bear-herd,[25] and now by present profession a tinker? Ask
Marian Hacket, the fat ale-wife[26] of Wincot, if she know   20
me not. If she say I am not fourteen pence on the score[27]
for sheer[28] ale, score me up for the lyingest knave[29] in
Christendom. What, I am not bestraught.[30] Here's –

Servant 3 O this it is that makes your lady mourn.
Servant 2 O this it is that makes your servants droop.   25
Lord   Hence[31] comes it, that your kindred shuns your house
As beaten[32] hence by your strange lunacy.
O noble lord, bethink[33] thee of thy birth,

15 such
16 reputation★
17 filled ("possessed")
18 attitude
19 would you = do you want to
20 insane
21 heath: uncultivated ground
22 traveling vendor, carrying wares in a sack
23 card: iron-teethed tool for separating and combing out fibers to be woven
    into fabric
24 transformation, change
25 bear keeper, leading a bear from place to place
26 female innkeeper
27 the score = account (kept by making marks – "scores" – on a stick, etc.)
28 neat, straight
29 rogue, fellow
30 distraught, out of one's mind
31 from this
32 driven
33 think about, recall, consider

Call home thy ancient[34] thoughts from banishment,
30 And banish hence these abject[35] lowly dreams.
Look how thy servants do attend on thee,
Each in his office ready at thy beck.[36]
Wilt thou have music? Hark, Apollo[37] plays,

MUSIC

And twenty cagèd nightingales do sing.
35 Or wilt thou sleep? We'll have[38] thee to a couch,[39]
Softer and sweeter than the lustful bed
On purpose trimmed up[40] for Semiramis.[41]
Say[42] thou wilt walk. We will bestrew the ground.
Or wilt thou ride? Thy horses shall be trapped,[43]
40 Their harness studded all with gold and pearl.
Dost thou love hawking? Thou hast hawks will soar
Above the morning lark. Or wilt thou hunt?
Thy hounds shall make the welkin[44] answer them
And fetch[45] shrill[46] echoes from the hollow earth.
45 *Servant 1* Say thou wilt course.[47] Thy greyhounds are as swift

34 former, bygone, old★
35 despicable, degraded, downcast
36 gesture of command
37 god of (among many, many other things) music
38 get, put, bring
39 bedlike resting furniture
40 trimmed up = readied, prepared
41 beautiful Assyrian queen (seMIRaMIS)
42 suppose, if
43 adorned
44 arch of heaven, sky
45 bring, cause to come
46 sharp, high-pitched
47 hunt with hounds

As breathèd[48] stags, ay, fleeter than the roe.[49]

Servant 2 Dost thou love pictures? We will fetch thee straight
Adonis[50] painted by[51] a running brook,
And Cytherea[52] all in sedges hid,[53]
Which seem to move and wanton[54] with her breath   50
Even as the waving sedges play with wind.

Lord   We'll show thee Io[55] as she was a maid[56]
And how she was beguilèd and surprised,
As lively[57] painted as the deed[58] was done.

Servant 3 Or Daphne[59] roaming through a thorny wood,   55
Scratching her legs, that[60] one shall swear[61] she bleeds,
And at that sight shall sad Apollo weep,
So workmanly[62] the blood and tears are drawn.

Lord   Thou art a lord, and nothing but a lord.
Thou hast a lady far more beautiful   60
Than any woman in this waning age.[63]

Servant 1 And till the tears that she hath shed for thee,

48 long-winded
49 species of small deer
50 beautiful prince and hunter, pursued by Venus (Cytherea)
51 near, alongside
52 Venus (KIthiREEa)
53 sedges hid = hidden in the rushes (spying on a naked Adonis)
54 play lasciviously
55 mythical princess, pursued by Zeus (EEo)
56 young, unmarried woman / virgin★
57 vividly ("realistically")
58 the deed = that which happened
59 nymph pursued by Apollo (DAFFnee)
60 so realistically that
61 would have to, must
62 skillfully
63 waning age = declining★ time

Like envious floods o'errun[64] her lovely face,

She was the fairest creature in the world,

65   And yet[65] she is inferior to[66] none.

Sly   Am I a lord, and have I such a lady?

Or do I dream? Or have I dreamed till now?

I do not sleep.[67] I see, I hear, I speak.

I smell sweet savors, and I feel soft things.

70   Upon my life I am a lord indeed,

And not a tinker, nor Christopher Sly.

Well, bring our[68] lady hither to our sight,

And once again, a pot o' th'smallest ale.

EXIT A SERVANT

Servant 2 Will't please your mightiness to wash your hands?

75   O how we joy to see your wit[69] restored,

O that once more you knew but[70] what you are.

These fifteen years you have been in a dream,

Or when you waked, so[71] waked as if you slept.

Sly   These fifteen years! By my fay,[72] a goodly[73] nap,

80   But did I never speak of[74] all that time?

Servant 1 O yes my lord, but very idle words,

For though you lay here in this goodly chamber,

---

64 floods o'errun = streams flowed over
65 still
66 inferior to = subordinate to, of lower rank than
67 I do not sleep = I'm not asleep
68 note the royal "we"
69 brain, mind
70 only, just
71 in the same way ("exactly")
72 faith
73 notable, good-sized★
74 during

Yet would you say, ye were beaten out of door,[75]
And rail upon[76] the hostess of the house,
And say you would present her[77] at the leet,[78]   85
Because she brought stone jugs,[79] and no sealed quarts.[80]
Sometimes you would call out for Cicely Hacket.[81]

Sly   Ay, the woman's maid of the house.[82]

Servant 3 Why sir, you know no house, nor no such maid,
Nor no such men as you have reckoned up,[83]   90
As Stephen Sly, and old John Naps of Greece,[84]
And Peter Turf, and Henry Pimpernell,
And twenty more such names and men as these,
Which never were, nor no man ever saw.

Sly   Now Lord be thankèd for my good amends![85]   95

All   Amen.

Sly   I thank thee, thou shalt not lose by[86] it.[87]

  ENTER PAGE, AS A LADY, WITH ATTENDANTS

Page How fares[88] my noble lord?

Sly   Marry[89] I fare well, for here is cheer[90] enough.

75 yet WOULD you SAY ye were BEAten OUT of DOOR
76 rail upon = curse★ at
77 present her = bring her before
78 manor (local) court
79 (which could be either adulterated or deficient in quantity)
80 (which could not be)
81 someTIMES you WOULD call OUT for SIsily HAckett
82 inn
83 reckoned up = listed, named
84 Greet, near Stafford
85 recovery
86 because of
87 I thank THEE thou SHALT not LOSE by IT
88 how fares = how is/does
89 exclamation of surprise (originally an invocation of Mary, Christ's mother)★
90 food and drink★

100 Where is my wife?

Page Here noble lord, what is thy will with her?

Sly Are you my wife, and will not call me husband?[91]

My men should[92] call me lord, I am your goodman.[93]

Page My husband and my lord, my lord and husband.

105 I am your wife in all obedience.

Sly I know it well. (*to Servants*) What must I call her?

Lord Madam.

Sly Al'ce[94] madam, or Joan madam?

Lord Madam, and nothing else, so lords call ladies.

110 *Sly* Madam wife, they say that I have dreamed

And slept above[95] some fifteen year or more.

Page Ay, and the time seems thirty unto me,

Being all this time abandoned[96] from your bed.

Sly 'Tis much.[97] Servants, leave me and her alone.

EXIT SERVANTS

115 Madam, undress you, and come now to bed.

Page Thrice noble lord, let me entreat of you

To pardon[98] me yet for a night or two.

Or, if not so, until the sun be set.

For your physicians have expressly charged

120 (In peril to incur[99] your former malady)

91 Sly is no fool; the page, not used to being "female," has in fact spoken
   incorrectly
92 must
93 husband
94 Alice (ALS: the vowel is swallowed)
95 more than
96 banished, expelled, cast out
97 a lot, important
98 excuse
99 in peril to incur = for the risk/danger of bringing on/falling back into

That I should yet absent[100] me from your bed.
I hope this reason stands for[101] my excuse.

Sly　　　Ay, it stands[102] so that I may hardly tarry[103] so long.
But I would be loath to fall into my dreams again. I will
therefore tarry, in despite of the flesh and the blood.　　　125

ENTER MESSENGER

Messenger　Your honor's players, hearing your amendment,[104]
Are come to play a pleasant comedy;
For so your doctors hold it very meet,[105]
Seeing too much sadness hath congealed[106] your blood,[107]
And melancholy is the nurse of frenzy,[108]　　　130
Therefore they thought it good you hear a play,
And frame[109] your mind to mirth and merriment,
Which bars[110] a thousand harms, and lengthens life.

Sly　　　Marry I will let them play. It is not a commonty,[111] a
Christmas gambol,[112] or a tumbling trick?[113]　　　135

Page　　　No my good lord, it is more pleasing stuff.[114]

Sly　　　What, household stuff?[115]

---

100 abSENT (verb)
101 stands for = upholds, supports, defends
102 it stands = his penis is erect
103 hardly tarry = with difficulty/painfully/barely wait/delay★
104 improvement, recovery
105 proper, appropriate, fitting★
106 curdled, thickened
107 seeing TOO much SADness HATH conGEALED your BLOOD
108 mental derangement, madness
109 (1) prepare, make ready, (2) direct, train★
110 prevents, blocks
111 mispronunciation of "comedy"
112 merry dance
113 tumbling trick = skillful acrobatic performance
114 material, substance
115 household stuff = domestic fooling about (sexual)

Page   It is a kind of history.[116]

Sly   Well, we'll see't.

   Come, madam wife, sit by my side

140   And let the world slip,[117] we shall ne'er be younger.

116 story, narrative
117 glide by

Act 1

𝔤

Padua. A street

ENTER LUCENTIO AND TRANIO

Lucentio Tranio, since for[1] the great desire I had
  To see fair Padua,[2] nursery of arts,[3]
  I am arrived for[4] fruitful[5] Lombardy,[6]
  The pleasant garden of great Italy,
  And by my father's love and leave[7] am armed
  With his good will, and thy good company.[8]   5
  My trusty servant well approved[9] in all,

---

1 since for = because of
2 PADyooa (trisyllabic)
3 scholarship, learning
4 in sight/the presence of
5 fertile, abundant
6 northern Italy, just S of Switzerland; the capital is Milan; and Padua, though in
   NE Italy, is not in Lombardy, but far to the E, relatively close to Venice
7 permission★ (to make this trip)
8 fellowship, companionship
9 tested, proven★

Here let us breathe,[10] and haply institute[11]
A course[12] of learning and ingenious[13] studies.
10   Pisa renownèd for grave[14] citizens
Gave[15] me my being, and my father first[16]
A merchant of great traffic[17] through the world,
Vincentio,[18] come of[19] the Bentivolii.[20]
Vincentio's son, brought up in Florence,
15   It shall become[21] to serve all[22] hopes conceived,[23]
To deck[24] his fortune[25] with his virtuous deeds.
And therefore Tranio, for the time I study,
Virtue and that part of philosophy
Will I apply,[26] that treats of[27] happiness,
20   By virtue specially to be achieved.
Tell me thy mind,[28] for I have Pisa left,
And am to Padua come, as[29] he that leaves

10 pause, rest
11 begin
12 path
13 liberal, high intellectual
14 important, influential*
15 "give" in the sense of "bestow, made" is syntactically implied for the father,
    later in this line
16 before that/me
17 profit ("business")
18 his father
19 descended from
20 in Italian, "loving"
21 it shall become = will properly come
22 all the
23 thought of, imagined
24 to deck = to clothe/adorn*
25 (1) good luck, (2) prosperity
26 devote myself to
27 treats of = deals with
28 thought, judgment, opinion
29 like

A shallow plash,[30] to plunge him in the deep,
And with satiety seeks to quench his thirst.
Tranio Mi perdonato,[31] gentle master mine.   25
   I am in all affected[32] as yourself,
   Glad that you thus continue your resolve
   To suck the sweets of sweet philosophy.
   Only, good master, while we do admire
   This virtue, and this moral discipline,   30
   Let's be no stoics,[33] nor no stocks[34] I pray,[35]
   Or so devote[36] to Aristotle's checks[37]
   As Ovid[38] be an outcast quite abjured.[39]
   Balk[40] logic with acquaintance[41] that you have,
   And practice rhetoric[42] in your common[43] talk.   35
   Music and poesy use,[44] to quicken you.
   The mathematics and the metaphysics
   Fall to[45] them as you find[46] your stomach serves[47] you.

30 pool of water
31 pardon / excuse me
32 inclined
33 Greek philosophical school, advocating non-emotional acceptance of
   whatever happens
34 blocks of wood
35 I pray = please★ ("I ask / request")
36 devote ourselves
37 restraints
38 that Ovid (famous for sensual, erotic verse)
39 quite abjured = entirely / wholly renounced / repudiated
40 bandy, quibble about
41 acquaintances
42 verbal eloquence (then – and for a long time before – considered a very
   important art)
43 general, public★
44 deal with★
45 fall to = consume, set to work on
46 discover, perceive★
47 stomach serves = appetite / desire★ leads you to / permits

No profit[48] grows, where is no pleasure ta'en.

40   In brief sir, study[49] what you most affect.

Lucentio Gramercies,[50] Tranio, well dost thou advise.

If, Biondello,[51] thou wert come ashore,

We could at once put us in readiness,

And take a lodging fit to entertain

45   Such friends as time in Padua shall beget.[52]

But stay awhile,[53] what company[54] is this?

Tranio   Master, some show[55] to welcome us to town.

LUCENTIO AND TRANIO STEP TO THE SIDE OF THE STAGE

ENTER BAPTISTA, KATHERINA, BIANCA, GREMIO,[56]
AND HORTENSIO

Baptista   Gentlemen, importune me no further,

For how I firmly am resolved[57] you know.

50   That is, not to bestow[58] my youngest daughter

Before I have a husband for the elder.

If either of you both[59] love Katherina,

Because I know you well and love you well,

---

48 advantage, benefit
49 learn★
50 thank you
51 if Biondello: Lucentio speaks as if addressing his other servant, Biondello, not
    yet disembarked
52 generate, produce
53 stay awhile = wait a minute/moment
54 group/party of people
55 public demonstration/procession/pageant (ironic?)
56 identified in the Folio stage direction as a "pantaloon," or clownlike old
    man
57 determined, settled, decided★
58 give, dispose of★
59 two

Leave shall you have to court her at your pleasure.[60]

Gremio   To cart[61] her rather. She's too rough[62] for me.   55

There, there, Hortensio, will you any wife?

Katherina[63] (to Baptista) I pray you, sir, is it your will

To make a stale[64] of me amongst these mates?[65]

Hortensio   Mates, maid, how mean you that? No mates[66] for you,

Unless you were of gentler, milder mold.[67]   60

Kate   I' faith, sir, you shall never need to fear,

Iwis[68] it is not halfway to[69] her[70] heart.

But if it were, doubt not, her care[71] should be

To comb your noddle[72] with a three-legged stool,

And paint[73] your face, and use you like a fool.   65

Hortensio   From all such devils, good Lord deliver us.

Gremio   And me, too, good Lord.

Tranio   Husht master, here's some good pastime toward.[74]

---

60 will, desire*
61 whores/bawds were drawn through the streets in a cart, and whipped as they
   went (note that Gremio is not speaking "aside," when he thus insults the
   young lady, but openly)
62 troublesome, violent, unreasonable*
63 hereafter "Kate"
64 whore, stuffed decoy bird, laughingstock
65 low-class males
66 husbands
67 nature
68 certainly, surely, truly
69 along the road to
70 my
71 concern
72 comb your noddle = beat/thrash your (empty) head
73 color with bruises/blood
74 pastime toward = amusement/entertainment coming (pasTIME
   toWARD)

That wench[75] is stark mad or wonderful froward.[76]

70 *Lucentio*   But in the other's silence do I see

Maid's mild[77] behavior and sobriety.[78]

Peace,[79] Tranio!

Tranio   Well said, master. Mum,[80] and gaze your fill.

Baptista   Gentlemen, that[81] I may soon make good[82]

75 What I have said, Bianca, get you in,

And let it not displease thee, good Bianca,

For I will love thee ne'er the less, my girl.

Kate   A pretty peat![83] It is best

Put finger in the eye,[84] an she knew why.

80 *Bianca*   Sister, content[85] you in my discontent.

Sir, to your pleasure humbly I subscribe.[86]

My books and instruments shall be my company,

On them to look, and practice[87] by myself.

Lucentio   Hark Tranio, thou mayst[88] hear Minerva[89] speak.

85 *Hortensio* Signior Baptista, will you be so strange?[90]

---

75 girl, young woman
76 wonderful froward = perverse / ungovernable / difficult★ (that WENCH is
   stark MAD or WONderFUL froWARD)
77 maid's mild = a virgin's gracious / gentle / conciliatory
78 seriousness, gravity
79 be still / silence★
80 be silent
81 in order that
82 make good = perform, fulfill, demonstrate
83 spoiled child, pet
84 put finger in the eye = make herself weep
85 be pleased / gratified★
86 yield, acquiesce
87 work, study
88 can (MAYist)
89 goddess of wisdom
90 cold, distant

Sorry am I that our good will effects[91]
Bianca's grief.
Gremio   Why will you mew[92] her up,
Signior Baptista, for[93] this fiend of hell,
And make her bear the penance[94] of her[95] tongue?
Baptista Gentlemen, content ye. I am resolved.   90
Go in, Bianca.

EXIT BIANCA

And for I know she taketh most delight
In music, instruments, and poetry,
Schoolmasters[96] will I keep within my house
Fit to instruct her youth. If you, Hortensio,   95
Or Signior Gremio, you know any such,
Prefer[97] them hither. For to cunning men
I will be very kind,[98] and liberal[99]
To mine own children in good bringing-up.
And so, farewell. Katherina, you may stay,[100]   100
For I have more to commune[101] with Bianca.[102]

EXIT BAPTISTA

91 good will effects = likings/pleasures cause/produce
92 confine, shut up, enclose
93 because/for the sake of
94 her bear the penance = Bianca suffer/endure the pain/distress/
    punishment
95 Kate's
96 private tutors
97 introduce, present, recommend
98 generous
99 unrestrained, gentlemanly
100 remain
101 discuss, talk about
102 for I have MORE to COMmune WITH biANca

Kate   Why, and I trust[103] I may go too, may I not?
What, shall I be appointed hours,[104] as though belike
I knew not what to take and what to leave? Ha!

EXIT KATE

105 *Gremio*   You may go to the devil's dam.[105] Your gifts[106] are so
good here's none[107] will hold[108] you. Their[109] love is not so
great,[110] Hortensio, but we may blow our nails together,[111]
and fast it fairly out.[112] Our cake's dough on both sides.[113]
Farewell. Yet for the love I bear[114] my sweet Bianca, if I can
110   by any means light on[115] a fit man to teach her that wherein
she delights, I will wish[116] him to her father.
Hortensio So will I, Signior Gremio. But a word, I pray. Though
the nature of our quarrel[117] yet never brooked parle,[118]

---

103 hope, believe, am confident
104 appointed hours = assigned/decreed regular/fixed times (for seeing her father)
105 mother
106 the things you offer
107 here's none = there's no one
108 keep from getting away, detain, stop
109 women's
110 important, critical
111 blow our nails together = do nothing, either one of us (like beggars out in the cold)
112 fast it fairly out = do without/abstain and get through it courteously/respectfully/impartially (with regard to their competition for Bianca)
113 our cake's dough on both sides = both of us have a loaf that isn't properly baked (neither of us having gotten Bianca)
114 feel/harbor for
115 light on = happen/chance upon, discover★
116 recommend
117 competitive unfriendliness
118 brooked parle = permitted discussion of the subject between us

know now upon advice[119] it toucheth[120] us both. That[121]
we may yet again have access to our fair mistress,[122] and be   115
happy rivals in Bianca's love, to[123] labor and effect one thing
specially.

Gremio   What's that, I pray?

Hortensio Marry, sir, to get a husband for her sister.

Gremio   A husband! A devil.   120

Hortensio   I say a husband.

Gremio   I say a devil. Thinkest thou, Hortensio, though her
father be very rich, any man is so very a fool to be married
to hell?

Hortensio Tush, Gremio. Though it pass your patience and mine   125
to endure[124] her loud alarums,[125] why man, there be good
fellows in the world, and[126] a man could light on them,
would take her with all faults, and money enough.

Gremio   I cannot tell.[127] But I had as lief[128] take her dowry[129]
with this condition: to be whipped at the high cross[130] every   130
morning.

Hortensio Faith, as you say, there's small choice in rotten apples.

119 on due consideration, after careful thought
120 is important, affects/concerns
121 in order that
122 lady love★
123 what we must both do is to
124 tolerate, withstand★
125 call to arms, sounds of impending battle
126 if
127 say
128 willingly, gladly
129 money/property given the husband by the wife's father
130 high cross = public cross, in markets/centers of town

But come, since this bar in law[131] makes us friends, it[132] shall
be so far forth[133] friendly maintained, till by helping
135   Baptista's eldest daughter to a husband, we set his youngest
free for a husband, and then have to't[134] afresh. Sweet Bianca,
happy man be his dole.[135] He that runs fastest, gets the ring.
How say you, Signior Gremio?

Gremio   I am agreed, and would[136] I had[137] given him the best
140   horse in Padua to begin his wooing, that[138] would
thoroughly[139] woo her, wed her, and bed her, and rid the
house of her. Come on.[140]

EXEUNT GREMIO AND HORTENSIO

Tranio   I pray sir, tell me, is it possible
That love should of a sudden take such hold?
145 *Lucentio* O Tranio, till I found it to be true,
I never thought it possible or likely.
But see, while idly[141] I stood looking on,
I found the effect[142] of love in idleness,
And now in plainness[143] do confess[144] to thee

---

131 bar in law = obstruction in what we are allowed to do (i.e., marry Bianca)
132 this friendship
133 so far forth = to that future point
134 have to't = fight, contend
135 happy man be his dole = the man who gets you as his lot in life / share /
    portion will be happy
136 wish
137 had already
138 so that he / the one who
139 absolutely and completely (and terminally)
140 come on = let's go
141 lazily
142 result, consequence
143 honesty, frankness★
144 declare, admit★

That[145] art to me as secret[146] and as dear   150
As Anna to the Queen of Carthage[147] was,
Tranio, I burn, I pine,[148] I perish,[149] Tranio,
If I achieve[150] not this young modest[151] girl.
Counsel me, Tranio, for I know thou canst.
Assist me, Tranio, for I know thou wilt.   155

Tranio   Master, it is no[152] time to chide[153] you now,
Affection is not rated[154] from the heart.
If love have touched you, nought remains but so:
Redime te captum quam queas minimo.[155]

Lucentio Gramercies, lad.[156] Go forward,[157] this contents,[158]   160
The rest will comfort, for thy counsel's sound.

Tranio   Master, you looked so longly[159] on the maid,
Perhaps you marked[160] not what's the pith[161] of all.

Lucentio O, yes, I saw sweet beauty in her face,

---

145 you who
146 intimate
147 queen of Carthage = Dido; Anna was her sister
148 suffer
149 will die/be destroyed/ruined
150 win
151 decorous, well-conducted, moderate
152 not a
153 scold★
154 reproved away from/out of
155 buy yourself out of bondage for the smallest possible price (Terence, but
        surely quoted, here, from a standard Elizabethan school text, *Lily's Grammar,*
        exposing the shallowness of the "Humanism" on display)
156 good fellow
157 on
158 conTENTS (verb)
159 at such length
160 noticed, observed★
161 central part

165   Such as the daughter of Agenor[162] had,

       That made great Jove to humble him[163] to her hand,

       When with his knees he kissed[164] the Cretan strand.[165]

Tranio   Saw you no more? Marked you not how her sister

       Began to scold and raise up such a storm

170   That mortal ears might hardly endure the din?

Lucentio Tranio, I saw her[166] coral[167] lips to move,

       And with her breath she did perfume the air.

       Sacred[168] and sweet was all I saw in her.

Tranio   (*aside*) (Nay, then 'tis time to stir him from his trance.)

175   I pray awake sir. If you love the maid,

       Bend[169] thoughts and wits to achieve her. Thus it stands:

       Her elder sister is so curst[170] and shrewd,[171]

       That till the father rid his hands of her,

       Master, your love must live a maid at home,

180   And therefore has he closely mewed her up,

       Because[172] she will not be annoyed with suitors.

Lucentio Ah, Tranio, what a cruel father's he.

       But art thou not advised,[173] he took some care

       To get her cunning schoolmasters to instruct her?

162 Europa (æGAYnor)
163 humble him = bow (verb)
164 with his knees he kissed = he knelt on
165 shore
166 Bianca's
167 red
168 holy
169 direct, turn, apply
170 damnable, awful, detestable★
171 (1) malicious, depraved, vile, harsh, (2) cursing, scolding, abusive
172 in order that
173 aware, informed

Tranio   Ay marry am I, sir – and now 'tis plotted.[174]   185
Lucentio I have it, Tranio.
Tranio   Master, for my hand,[175]
   Both our inventions[176] meet and jump[177] in one.
Lucentio Tell me thine first.
Tranio   You will be schoolmaster,
   And undertake the teaching of the maid.
   That's your device.[178]
Lucentio   It is. May it be done?   190
Tranio   Not possible. For who shall bear[179] your part,
   And be in Padua here Vincentio's son,
   Keep house, and ply[180] his book,[181] welcome his friends,
   Visit his countrymen, and banquet them?
Lucentio Basta,[182] content thee. For I have it full.[183]   195
   We have not yet been seen in any house,
   Nor can we be distinguished by our faces,
   For man[184] or master. Then it follows thus:
   Thou shalt be master, Tranio, in my stead,
   Keep[185] house, and port,[186] and servants, as I should.   200
   I will some other be, some Florentine,

174 all planned/arranged
175 for my hand = I dare say, I suspect
176 solutions, creations, plans, schemes
177 agree exactly/completely
178 design, plan
179 maintain/carry
180 work busily at, apply oneself to★
181 books
182 enough
183 have it full = have it completely worked out
184 servant
185 attend to the
186 behavior, style of life★

Some Neapolitan, or meaner[187] man of Pisa.
'Tis hatched,[188] and shall be so. Tranio, at once
Uncase[189] thee. Take my colored hat and cloak.[190]
205 When Biondello comes, he waits on[191] thee,
But I will charm[192] him first to keep his tongue.

THEY EXCHANGE CLOTHES

Tranio   So had you need.
In brief, sir, sith[193] it your pleasure is,
And I am tied[194] to be obedient,
210 For so your father charged me at our parting:
"Be serviceable[195] to my son," quoth[196] he,
Although I think 'twas in another sense.
I am content to be Lucentio,
Because so well I love Lucentio.
215 *Lucentio* Tranio, be so, because Lucentio loves,
And let me be a slave, t'achieve that maid,
Whose sudden sight hath thralled[197] my wounded[198] eye.

ENTER BIONDELLO

187 lower ranked, inferior★
188 fully developed
189 undress (outer garments)
190 my colored hat and cloak: Lucentio is a master, and therefore dresses
   vibrantly; Tranio is a servant, and wears garments of dark blue or some such
   relatively drab hue
191 waits on = serves
192 control, influence, as by a magical charm★
193 since
194 bound
195 ready to serve/be useful (SERviSAble)
196 said (quoth: present tense, though the meaning, in modern usage, is past
   tense)
197 taken captive, enslaved
198 i.e., by Cupid's love-arrow

Here comes the rogue. Sirrah, where have you been?

Biondello Where have I been?[199] Nay, how now? Where are
you?[200]

Master, has my fellow[201] Tranio stol'n your clothes,   220

Or you stol'n his, or both? Pray, what's the news?

Lucentio   Sirrah, come hither, 'tis no time to jest,

And therefore frame your manners to the time.

Your fellow Tranio here, to save my life,

Puts my apparel and my count'nance[202] on,   225

And I for my escape have put on his.

For in a quarrel since I came ashore

I killed a man, and fear I was descried.[203]

Wait you on him, I charge you, as becomes,[204]

While I make way[205] from hence to save my life.   230

You understand me?

Biondello   I, sir! Ne'er a whit.[206]

Lucentio   And not a jot[207] of Tranio in your mouth,[208]

Tranio is chang'd into[209] Lucentio.

Biondello The better for him, would I were so too.

Tranio   So could I, faith, boy, to have the next wish[210] after,[211]   235

199 he thinks, at first, that Tranio is speaking
200 looking for Tranio
201 co-worker
202 appearance, behavior
203 observed
204 appropriate, suitable, fitting★
205 away
206 bit
207 bit
208 either Lucentio (1) hears "Ay, sir," or (2) knows Biondello and ignores his
   jesting
209 inTO
210 are second wishes, like second thoughts, superior?
211 so COULD i FAITH boy to HAVE the NEXT wish AFter (not good

That Lucentio indeed had Baptista's youngest daughter.
But sirrah, not for my sake, but your master's, I advise
You use your manners discreetly in all kind of companies.
When I am alone, why then I am Tranio.

240 But in all places else, your[212] master, Lucentio.

Lucentio   Tranio, let's go.
One thing more rests,[213] that thyself execute,[214]
To make one among these wooers. If thou ask me why,
Sufficeth my reasons are both good and weighty.[215]

EXEUNT

THE ACTORS FROM THE INTRODUCTION,
STILL WATCHING FROM ABOVE, SPEAK

245 *Servant 1*   My lord you nod, you do not mind[216] the play.

Sly   Yes by Saint Anne[217] do I, a good matter, surely.
Comes there any more of it?

Page   My lord 'tis but begun.

Sly   'Tis a very excellent piece of work, Madame Lady.

250 Would 'twere done.

THEY SIT AND WATCH

---

poetry: the Folio prints this Tranio-Biondello dialogue as prose; most
    editors have chosen verse)
212 I am your
213 remains
214 carry into effect ("do")
215 significant, important*
216 attend/pay attention to
217 the Virgin Mary's mother

SCENE 2

Outside Hortensio's house

<small>ENTER PETRUCHIO[1] AND HIS PERSONAL SERVANT, GRUMIO</small>

Petruchio Verona, for a while I take my leave,
  To see my friends in Padua, but of all[2]
  My best belovèd and approvèd friend,
  Hortensio – and I trow[3] this is his house.
  Here sirrah Grumio, knock I say.   5

Grumio Knock[4] sir? Whom should I knock? Is there any man
  has rebused[5] your worship?

Petruchio Villain,[6] I say, knock me here[7] soundly.

Grumio Knock you here sir! Why sir, what am I,[8] sir, that I
  should knock you here sir?   10

Petruchio Villain, I say, knock me at this gate,
  And rap me well, or I'll knock your knave's pate.[9]

Grumio My master is grown quarrelsome. I should knock you
  first,
  And then I know after who comes by the worst.[10]

Petruchio Will it not be?   15
  'Faith, sirrah, an you'll not knock, I'll ring[11] it,

1 peTROOcheeO
2 of all = first of all
3 (1) believe, am confident, (2) imagine, suppose★
4 (1) rap on a door, (2) beat, punch
5 abused? (Abbott and Costello farce)
6 peasant, low-born rustic★
7 wordplay on me here/me ear : (1) reflexive, (2) Cockney dropping of initial
  "h" sound
8 what am I = what sort/kind of man ("who")
9 head, noggin
10 who comes by the worst: "me," suggests Grumio; "you're setting me up"
11 wordplay on ring/wring (wring = twist, squeeze)

I'll try[12] how you can sol, fa,[13] and sing it.

PETRUCHIO WRINGS GRUMIO BY THE EARS

Grumio Help, mistress,[14] help, my master is mad.
Petruchio Now knock when I bid you, sirrah villain!

ENTER HORTENSIO

20 *Hortensio* How now, what's the matteer? My old friend Grumio,
     and my good friend Petruchio? How do you all at Verona?
    Petruchio Signior Hortensio, come you to part the fray?[15]
     Con tutto il cuore ben trovato,[16] may I say.
    Hortensio Alla nostra casa ben venuto, molto honorato signor mio
25   *Petruchio.*[17]
     Rise, Grumio, rise, we will compound[18] this quarrel.
    Grumio Nay, 'tis no matter, sir, what he 'leges[19] in Latin.[20] If
     this be not a lawful cause[21] for me to leave his service, look
     you, sir. He bid me knock him and rap him soundly, sir. Well,
30   was it fit for a servant to use his master so, being perhaps for
     aught I see two-and-thirty, a peep out?[22]

---

12 test, find out★
13 sol, fa = do, re, me, sol, fa
14 commonly emended to "masters," but on no authority: it is just as likely that
   Grumio seeks help from the mistress of the house as from masters (other
   men of his own social level)
15 disturbance, noisy quarrel, fight
16 with all my heart well met
17 welcome to our/my house, much honored Signior Petruchio
18 settle
19 alleges: swears to
20 Grumio's language, like that of the play, is English, and as an uneducated man
   he cannot tell one foreign tongue from another
21 reason★
22 Petruchio is (1) more or less aged 32, and too old for a younger man to fight
   with, (2) drunk (one-and-thirty = drunk), a meaning drawn from "pip,"

Whom would to God I had well knocked at first,

Then had not Grumio come by the worst.

Petruchio   A senseless villain! Good Hortensio,

I bade the rascal knock upon your gate,   35

And could not get him for my heart to do it.

Grumio   Knock at the gate? O heavens! Spake you not these

words plain? "Sirrah knock me here, rap me here, knock me

well, and knock me soundly?" And come you now with

"knocking at the gate"?   40

Petruchio   Sirrah be gone, or talk not I advise you.

Hortensio   Petruchio, patience. I am Grumio's pledge.[23]

Why, this's[24] a heavy chance[25] 'twixt him and you,

Your ancient, trusty, pleasant[26] servant Grumio.

And tell me now, sweet friend, what happy gale   45

Blows you to Padua here from old Verona?

Petruchio   Such wind as scatters young men through the world,

To seek their fortunes farther than at home,

Where small experience grows.[27] But in a few,[28]

Signior Hortensio, thus it stands with me: 50

Antonio my father is deceased,

And I have thrust myself into this maze,[29]

---

which is also a form of "peep," to which word many editors emend, (3) in
the card game Trente et un, "Thirty-One" [like "Black Jack," a form of
poker, in which the player aims for a total of 21], to have your cards add up to
more than 31 is to lose the hand

23 bail, guarantee

24 the Folio's "this" is almost always emended to "this's"

25 heavy chance = serious/grave★ occurrence/event/accident★

26 merry, cheerful

27 the Folio has no punctuation here and ends the sentence after "a few"; every
editor emends

28 in a few = briefly, in a few words

29 confused wandering (the world as labyrinth)

Haply to wive and thrive, as best I may.
Crowns[30] in my purse I have, and goods[31] at home,
55   And so am come abroad[32] to see the world.
    Hortensio Petruchio, shall I then come roundly[33] to thee
    And wish thee to a shrewed ill-favored[34] wife?
    Thou'dst[35] thank me but a little for my counsel,
    And yet I'll promise thee she shall be rich,
60   And very rich. But th'art too much my friend,
    And I'll not wish thee to her.
    Petruchio Signor Hortensio, 'twixt such friends as we
    Few words suffice. And therefore, if thou know
    One rich enough to be Petruchio's wife,
65   As wealth is burden[36] of my wooing dance,
    Be she as foul[37] as was Florentius'[38] love,
    As old as Sibyl,[39] and as curst and shrewd
    As Socrates' Xanthippe[40] or a worse.
    She moves[41] me not, or not removes at least
70   Affection's edge[42] in me, were she as rough

30 gold coins
31 property, possessions★
32 away from home
33 plainly, directly, bluntly★
34 bad / harsh / malicious-natured
35 you'd
36 (1) accompaniment, (2) chief theme
37 ugly
38 legendary knight betrothed to a haggish old woman; she turns into a
   beautiful young girl once the man concedes her the power to govern him
   (floRENshusiz)
39 the Cumae Sibyl, or prophetess, to whom Apollo gave as many years as grains
   of sand in her hand
40 Socrates' legendarily shrewish wife (zanTIpee)
41 provokes, affects★
42 force, power, ardor

As are the swelling Adriatic seas.

I come to wive it wealthily in Padua.

If wealthily, then happily in Padua.

Grumio   (*to Hortensio*) Nay look you, sir, he tells you flatly what   75
his mind is. Why give him gold enough and marry him to a
puppet[43] or an aglet-baby,[44] or an old trot[45] with ne'er a
tooth in her head, though she has as many diseases as two-
and-fifty horses. Why nothing comes amiss,[46] so money
comes withal.[47]

Hortensio Petruchio, since we are stepped[48] thus far in,   80
I will continue that[49] I broached[50] in jest.
I can, Petruchio, help[51] thee to a wife
With wealth enough, and young and beauteous,
Brought up as best becomes a gentlewoman.
Her only fault, and that is faults enough,   85
Is, that she is intolerable curst,
And shrewd, and froward, so beyond all measure
That, were my state[52] far worser than it is,
I would not wed her for a mine[53] of gold.

Petruchio Hortensio, peace, thou know'st not gold's effect.   90
Tell me her father's name, and 'tis enough.

---

43 dressed-up doll of a woman (poppet)
44 spangle-adorned doll
45 hag
46 comes amiss = happens erroneously/faultily/wrongly★
47 along with the rest, in addition, moreover★
48 are stepped = have gone forward
49 that which
50 introduced, began
51 assist★
52 condition★
53 great mass

For I will board[54] her, though she chide as loud

As thunder, when the clouds in autumn crack.[55]

Hortensio Her father is Baptista Minola,

95   An affable[56] and courteous gentleman.

Her name is Katherina Minola,

Renowned in Padua for her scolding tongue.

Petruchio I know her father, though I know not her,

And he knew my deceasèd father well.

100   I will not sleep Hortensio, till I see her,

And therefore let me be thus bold with you,

To give you over[57] at this first encounter,

Unless you will accompany me thither.

Grumio   (*to Hortensio*) I pray you, sir, let him go[58] while the

105   humor lasts. A[59] my word, an she knew him as well as I do,

she would think scolding would do little good upon him. She

may perhaps call him half a score knaves, or so. Why, that's

nothing. And he begin once, he'll rail[60] in his rope-tricks.[61]

I'll tell you what sir, an she stand him[62] but a little, he will

110   throw a figure[63] in her face, and so disfigure her with it, that

she shall have no more eyes to see withal than a cat. You

know him not sir.

Hortensio Tarry Petruchio, I must go with thee,

---

54 approach, make advances to (as attackers board a ship)
55 make a sharp noise
56 civil, courteous★
57 give you over = leave / abandon / desert you
58 polite guests asked their host's leave before departing
59 on
60 rattle along
61 rope-tricks = rhetoric (as the word is mangled by Grumio)
62 stand him = hold her ground against / resist / withstand him
63 rhetorical figure (way of expression)

For in Baptista's keep[64] my treasure is.
He hath the jewel of my life in hold,[65]   115
His youngest daughter, beautiful Bianca,
And her withholds from me and[66] other more
Suitors to her, and rivals in my love,
Supposing it a thing impossible,
For those defects I have before rehearsed,   120
That ever Katherina will be wooed.
Therefore this order[67] hath Baptista ta'en,[68]
That none shall have access unto Bianca
Till Katherine the curst have got a husband.

Grumio   Katherine the curst!   125
A title[69] for a maid of all titles the worst.

Hortensio Now shall my friend Petruchio do me grace,[70]
And offer me disguised in sober robes,
To old Baptista as a schoolmaster
Well seen[71] in music, to instruct Bianca,   130
That so I may, by this device at least
Have leave and leisure to make love to[72] her,
And unsuspected court her by herself.

Grumio   Here's no knavery. See, to beguile the old folks, how
the young folks lay their heads together.   135

---

64 (1) care, custody, (2) castle
65 in hold = in his stronghold
66 not in the Folio: all editors emend
67 arrangement, sequence★
68 hit upon, adopted
69 label, name
70 do me grace = set me in a good/honorable light
71 versed
72 make love to = court

ENTER GREMIO AND LUCENTIO, DISGUISED,
CARRYING BOOKS

Master, master, look about you. Who goes there, ha?

Hortensio Peace, Grumio. 'Tis the rival of my love.

Petruchio, stand by[73] awhile.

Grumio   A proper stripling,[74] and an amorous.

140 *Gremio*   (*to Lucentio*) O very well,[75] I have perused the note.[76]

Hark you sir, I'll have them very fairly bound,[77]

All books of love, see that at any hand,[78]

And see you read no other lectures[79] to her.

You understand me. Over and beside

145 Signior Baptista's liberality,

I'll mend[80] it with a largess.[81] Take your paper[82] too,

And let me have them[83] very well perfumed,

For she is sweeter than perfume itself

To whom they go to. What will you read to her?[84]

150 *Lucentio*   Whate'er I read to her, I'll plead for you,

As for my patron, stand[85] you so assured,

---

73 stand by = step aside (to the side of the stage)
74 proper stripling = handsome young fellow (spoken – sarcastically – of Gremio)
75 very well = very good
76 written description, in this case a reading list for Bianca
77 Gremio proposes to purchase the books for Bianca; books were not usually available already bound, and expensive bindings were a mark of ostentatious wealth
78 see that at any hand = see to that in any case
79 written works
80 improve★
81 bountifulness, munificence
82 the written list
83 the books
84 that is, in addition to the books she herself reads
85 remain, continue

As firmly as[86] yourself were still in place,[87]
Yea, and perhaps with more successful words
Than you, unless you were a scholar,[88] sir.

Gremio   O this learning, what a thing it is.   155
Grumio   O this woodcock,[89] what an ass it is.
Petruchio   Peace, sirrah.
Hortensio   Grumio, mum.

> HORTENSIO COMES FORWARD, PETRUCHIO
> AND GREMIO FOLLOW

God save you,[90] Signior Gremio.

Gremio   And you are well met, Signior Hortensio.
Trow you whither I am going? To Baptista Minola.   160
I promised to inquire carefully
About a schoolmaster for the fair Bianca,
And by good fortune[91] I have lighted well
On this young man, for learning and behavior
Fit for her turn,[92] well read in poetry   165
And other books, good ones, I warrant ye.

Hortensio   'Tis well. And I have met a gentleman
Hath promised me to help me to another,
A fine musician to instruct our mistress,
So shall I no whit be behind in duty   170
To fair Bianca, so beloved of me.

---

86 as if
87 still in place = always there
88 (1) a student,★ (2) a university student (as he himself has presumably been)
89 fool, simpleton, dupe
90 God save you = may you achieve salvation (conventional greeting)★
91 luck★
92 condition, state, circumstances★

Gremio	Beloved of me, and that my deeds shall prove.
Grumio	(*aside*) And that his bags[93] shall prove.
Hortensio	Gremio, 'tis now no time to vent[94] our love.

175   Listen to me, and if you speak me fair,[95]

I'll tell you news indifferent[96] good for either.[97]

Here is a gentleman whom by chance I met,

Upon agreement from us to his liking

Will undertake to woo curst Katherine,

180   Yea, and to marry her, if her dowry please.

Gremio   So said, so done, is well.

Hortensio, have you told him all her faults?

Petruchio I know she is an irksome brawling scold.

If that be all, masters,[98] I hear no harm.

185 Gremio   No, say'st me so, friend? What countryman?

Petruchio Born in Verona, old Antonio's son.

My father dead, my fortune lives for me,[99]

And I do hope, good days and long to see.

Gremio   O sir, such a life, with such a wife, were strange!

190   But if you have a stomach, to't a'[100] God's name,

You shall have me assisting you in all.

But will you woo this wildcat?

Petruchio   Will I live?

---

93 bags of money

94 express, make known

95 speak me fair = speak to me agreeably/courteously

96 impartially, even-handedly★

97 either of us

98 sirs★

99 in 2.1.000 Petruchio says that he has "bettered rather than decreased" what his father left him

100 to't a' = go to it/ahead, in

Grumio   (*aside*) Will he woo her? Ay. Or I'll hang her.

Petruchio   Why came I hither but to that intent?[101]

Think you a little din[102] can daunt[103] mine ears?   195

Have I not in my time heard lions roar?

Have I not heard the sea, puffed up with winds,

Rage like an angry boar, chafed with sweat?[104]

Have I not heard great ordnance[105] in the field?

And heaven's artillery thunder in the skies?   200

Have I not in a pitchèd[106] battle heard

Loud 'larums,[107] neighing steeds, and trumpets' clang?

And do you tell me of a woman's tongue?

That gives not half so great a blow to hear

As will a chestnut in a farmer's fire?   205

Tush, tush, fear boys with bugs.

Grumio   (*aside*) For he fears none.[108]

Gremio   Hortensio, hark.

This gentleman is happily[109] arrived,

My mind presumes, for his own good and yours.[110]

Hortensio I promised we would be contributors,   210

And bear his charge[111] of wooing whatsoe'er.

---

101 purpose, intention
102 loud noise
103 conquer, tame, discourage
104 chafed with sweat = raging/hot/irritated★ with blood
105 cannons
106 full-scale
107 see "alarums," I.1.n125
108 no one
109 (1) see haply, or (2) fortunately
110 many editors emend to "ours"; the Folio "yours" is confirmed by the
    subsequent comments of both Hortensio and Grumio, indicating that
    Gremio is strongly suspected of welching
111 expense

Gremio	And so we will, provided that he win her.
Grumio	(*aside*) I would I were as sure of a good dinner.

ENTER TRANIO, DRESSED AS LUCENTIO, AND BIONDELLO

	Tranio	Gentlemen, God save you. If I may be bold,[112]
215		Tell me, I beseech[113] you, which is the readiest way[114]
		To the house of Signior Baptista Minola?
	Biondello	He that has the two fair daughters. Is't he you mean?
	Tranio:	Even he, Biondello.
	Gremio	Hark you sir, you mean not her to –
220	*Tranio*	Perhaps him and her, sir. What have you to do?[115]
	Petruchio	Not her that chides sir, at any hand, I pray.
	Tranio	I love no chiders[116] sir. Biondello, let's away.
	Lucentio	(*aside*) Well begun, Tranio.
	Hortensio	Sir, a word ere[117] you go.
		Are you a suitor to the maid you talk of, yea or no?
225	*Tranio*	And if I be sir, is it any offense?
	Gremio	No. If without more words you will get you hence.
	Tranio	Why sir, I pray are not the streets as free
		For me as for you?
	Gremio	But so is not she.[118]
	Tranio	For what reason, I beseech you?
230	*Gremio*	For this reason, if you'll[119] know,

112 be bold = presume, take the liberty
113 earnestly request★
114 readiest way = most convenient road/path★
115 to do = to do with it★ ("what business is it of yours?")
116 quarrelsome people
117 before★
118 Bianca
119 you'll = you will = you want to

That she's the choice love of Signior Gremio.

Hortensio   That she's the chosen of Signior Hortensio.

Tranio   Softly[120] my masters. If you be gentlemen
Do me this right.[121] Hear me with patience.
Baptista is a noble gentleman,   235
To whom my father is not all unknown,
And were his daughter fairer than she is,
She may more suitors have, and me for one.
Fair Leda's daughter[122] had a thousand wooers,
Then well one more may fair Bianca have,   240
And so she shall. Lucentio shall make one,
Though Paris[123] came,[124] in hope to speed[125] alone.

Gremio   What, this gentleman will out-talk us all.

Lucentio   Sir, give him head,[126] I know he'll prove a jade.[127]

Petruchio   Hortensio, to what end[128] are all these words?   245

Hortensio   Sir, let me be so bold as ask you,
Did you yet ever see Baptista's daughter?

Tranio   No sir, but hear I do that he hath two,
The one, as famous for a scolding tongue,
As is the other for beauteous modesty.   250

Petruchio   Sir, sir, the first's for me, let her go by.

Gremio   Yea, leave that labor to great Hercules,

---

120 slowly, gently★
121 justice
122 Helen of Troy
123 who brought Helen to Troy and thereby began the Greek-Trojan war
124 were to come
125 succeed, prosper★
126 give him head = let him hurry/race on
127 a worthless horse★ (who'll soon grow tired)
128 purpose, result

And let it be more than Alcides'[129] twelve.

Petruchio Sir understand you this of me, in sooth.[130]

255 The youngest daughter, whom you hearken[131] for,

Her father keeps from all access[132] of suitors,

And will not promise her to any man

Until the elder sister first be wed.

The younger then is free, and not before.

260 *Tranio* If it be so sir, that you are the man

Must stead[133] us all, and me amongst the rest,

And if you break the ice, and do this feat,

Achieve the elder, set the younger free

For our access, whose hap[134] shall be to have her

265 Will not so graceless be, to be ingrate.[135]

Hortensio Sir you say well, and well you do conceive,[136]

And since you do profess[137] to be a suitor,

You must, as we do, gratify[138] this gentleman,

To whom we all rest generally beholding.[139]

270 *Tranio* Sir, I shall not be slack. In sign whereof,

Please ye we may contrive[140] this afternoon,

129 the name, meaning "descendant of Alcaeus," was another way of referring
to Hercules (who had twelve virtually impossible labors to perform)
(alSEEdeez)
130 truth*
131 ask
132 akSESS
133 be of use/advantage to, help
134 fortune, luck
135 ungrateful (inGRATE)
136 understand, imagine, comprehend
137 declare, affirm
138 reward, remunerate
139 rest generally beholding = remain as a group under obligation*
140 pass time

And quaff carouses[141] to our mistress' health,
And do as adversaries do in law,[142]
Strive mightily, but eat and drink as friends.
Grumio, Biondello O excellent motion.[143] Fellows, let's be gone.   275
Hortensio The motion's good indeed, and be it so,
Petruchio, I shall be your *ben venuto*.[144]

EXEUNT

141 quaff carouses = drink deep/repeated/continuous toasts
142 adversaries ... in law = lawyers on opposing sides
143 suggestion, proposal
144 host, welcomer

Act 2

𝔅

SCENE I

Baptista's house

ENTER KATHERINA AND BIANCA, TIED UP

Bianca Good sister wrong me not, nor wrong yourself,
  To make a bondmaid[1] and a slave of me,
  That I disdain.[2] But for[3] these other gawds,[4]
  Unbind my hands, I'll[5] pull them off myself,
5 Yea, all my raiment, to[6] my petticoat,
  Or what[7] you will command me will I do,
  So well I know my duty to my elders.
Kate Of all thy suitors here I charge thee[8] tell
  Whom thou lov'st best. See[9] thou dissemble[10] not.

1 to make a bondmaid = by making an indentured servant/slave
2 am offended by/angry at
3 but for = as for
4 showy ornaments, gewgaws (Folio: goods; most editors emend)
5 and I'll
6 down to/as far as
7 whatever
8 not in the Folio; all editors emend
9 watch out, take care
10 deceive, pretend

54

Bianca   Believe me, sister, of all the men alive   10
     I never yet beheld that special face
     Which I could fancy[11] more than any other.
Kate   Minion,[12] thou liest. Is't not Hortensio?
Bianca   If you affect[13] him sister, here I swear
     I'll plead for you myself, but you shall have him.   15
Kate   O then belike you fancy riches more,
     You will[14] have Gremio to keep you fair.
Bianca   Is it for him you do envy[15] me so?
     Nay then you jest, and now I well perceive
     You have but jested with me all this while.   20
     I prithee[16] sister Kate, untie my hands.

KATE STRIKES HER

Kate   If that be jest, then all the rest was so.[17]

ENTER BAPTISTA

Baptista (*to Kate*) Why how now dame,[18] whence grows this
     insolence?[19]
     Bianca, stand aside. Poor girl she weeps.
     (*unties her*) Go ply thy needle, meddle[20] not with her.   25
     (*to Kate*) For shame, thou hilding[21] of a devilish spirit,

11 like, love★
12 hussy, slave
13 are drawn to, love
14 wish to
15 to be jealous of, dislike (enVIE: rhymes with "eye," "high," "sky," etc.)
16 pray you★
17 exactly the same
18 lady
19 haughtiness, overbearing conduct/disposition
20 associate, mix, concern yourself
21 jade, baggage

Why dost thou wrong her, that did ne'er wrong thee?
When did she cross[22] thee with a bitter word?

Kate   Her silence flouts[23] me, and I'll be revenged.

SPRINGS AT BIANCA

30 *Baptista* What, in my sight? Bianca, get thee in.

EXIT BIANCA

Kate   What, will you not suffer[24] me? Nay now I see
She is your treasure, she must have a husband,
I must dance barefoot on her wedding day,[25]
And for[26] your love to her, lead[27] apes in hell.[28]
35   Talk not to me, I will go sit and weep
Till I can find occasion of[29] revenge.

EXIT KATE

Baptista Was ever gentleman thus grieved[30] as I?
But who comes here?

ENTER GREMIO, WITH LUCENTIO IN COMMONER CLOTHING,
PETRUCHIO, HORTENSIO AS MUSICIAN, TRANIO,
AND BIONDELLO CARRYING A LUTE AND BOOKS

Gremio   Good morrow,[31] neighbor Baptista.

---

22 oppose, go against★
23 mocks, insults, shows contempt for
24 put up with, tolerate, endure
25 unmarried older sisters danced barefoot at a younger sister's wedding, hoping thereby to catch themselves a husband
26 because of
27 must lead
28 lead apes in hell: what old maids were thought to do, after death
29 occasion of = an opportunity for
30 harassed, oppressed, afflicted
31 good morrow = I wish you a good morning/day ("hello")★

Baptista   Good morrow, neighbor Gremio. God save you,
    gentlemen.   40

Petruchio And you[32] good sir. Pray, have you not a daughter,
    Called Katherina, fair and virtuous?[33]

Baptista   I have a daughter sir, called Katherina.

Gremio   (*to Petruchio*) You are too blunt, go to it orderly.[34]

Petruchio (*to Gremio*) You wrong[35] me, Signior Gremio, give me
    leave.   45

    (*to Baptista*) I am a gentleman of Verona, sir,

    That hearing of her beauty, and her wit,

    Her affability and bashful modesty,

    Her wondrous qualities and mild behavior,

    Am bold to show myself a forward[36] guest   50

    Within your house, to make mine eye the witness

    Of that report, which I so oft have heard,

    And for an entrance[37] to my entertainment,[38]

    I do present you with a man[39] of mine

    (*presents Hortensio*) Cunning in music, and the mathematics,   55

    To instruct her fully in those sciences,[40]

    Whereof I know she is not ignorant.

    Accept of[41] him, or else you do me wrong.

    His name is Litio,[42] born in Mantua.

32 the same to you
33 CALLED kaTRIna FAIR and VIRtuOUS
34 in due order, properly
35 are unfair/disrespectful
36 eager, ardent★
37 entrance fee, ticket of admission
38 reception★
39 servant
40 bodies of knowledge
41 accept of = receive
42 in modern Italian, this would be Lisio

60   *Baptista*   You're welcome sir, and he for your good sake.

But for my daughter Katherine, this I know,

She is not for your turn, the more my grief.

Petruchio I see you do not mean to part with her,

Or else you like not of[43] my company.

65   *Baptista*   Mistake me not, I speak but as I find.

Whence are you sir? What may I call your name?

Petruchio Petruchio is my name, Antonio's son,

A man well known throughout all Italy.

Baptista   I know him well. You are welcome for his sake.

70   *Gremio*   Saving[44] your tale, Petruchio, I pray

Let us that are poor petitioners speak too?

Backare,[45] you are marvellous forward.

Petruchio O, pardon me, Signior Gremio, I would fain[46] be

doing.[47]

Gremio   I doubt it not, sir, but you will curse your wooing.

75   (*to Baptista*) Neighbor, this is a gift very grateful,[48] I am sure

of it. To express the like kindness, myself, that[49] have been

more kindly beholding to you than any, freely give unto you

this young scholar (*presenting Lucentio*) that has been long

studying at Rheims,[50] as cunning in Greek, Latin, and other

80   languages, as the other[51] in music and mathematics. His name

is Cambio. Pray accept his service.

---

43 like not of = do not care for
44 meaning no offense to
45 stand back, make room (the word looks, but does not seem to be, Italian)
46 rejoice, be glad
47 (1) active, (2) having sexual intercourse
48 pleasing, acceptable, welcome
49 I who
50 ancient French university (RANCE)
51 Hortensio/Litio

Baptista   A thousand thanks, Signior Gremio. Welcome, good
   Cambio. (*to Tranio*) But gentle sir, methinks you walk like a
   stranger. May I be so bold to[52] know the cause of your
   coming?   85

Tranio   Pardon me sir, the boldness is mine own,
   That being a stranger in this city here,
   Do make myself a suitor to your daughter,
   Unto Bianca, fair and virtuous.
   Nor is your firm resolve unknown to me,   90
   In the preferment[53] of the eldest sister.
   This liberty is all that I request,
   That upon knowledge of my parentage,
   I may have welcome 'mongst the rest that woo,
   And free access and favor as[54] the rest.   95
   And toward the education of your daughters,
   I here bestow a simple instrument,[55]
   And this small packet of Greek and Latin books.
   If you accept them, then their worth is great.

Baptista (*peering into books*) Lucentio is your name? Of   100
   whence,[56] I pray?

Tranio   Of Pisa, sir, son to Vincentio.

Baptista A mighty man of Pisa, by report,
   I know him well. You are very welcome, sir.
   (*to Hortensio*) Take you the lute, (*to Lucentio*) and you the set of
   books.

---

52 as to
53 prior status
54 the same as
55 the lute that Biondello had been carrying
56 of whence = from where

105 You shall go see your pupils presently.[57]
Holla,[58] within!

ENTER SERVANT

Sirrah, lead these gentlemen
To my daughters, and tell them both
These are their tutors, bid them[59] use them[60] well.

EXEUNT SERVANT, HORTENSIO, LUCENTIO, AND BIONDELLO

We will go walk a little in the orchard,[61]
110 And then to dinner. You are passing welcome,
And so[62] I pray you all to think yourselves.
Petruchio Signior Baptista, my business asketh haste,
And every day I cannot come to woo.
You knew my father well, and in him me,
115 Left solely heir to all his lands and goods,
Which I have bettered rather than decreased.
Then tell me, if I get your daughter's love,
What dowry shall I have with her to wife?
Baptista After my death, the one half of my lands,
120 And in possession[63] twenty thousand crowns.[64]
Petruchio And for that dowry, I'll assure her of
Her widowhood, be it that she survive me,
In all my lands and leases whatsoever.

57 at once, now
58 exclamation, used to get someone's attention★
59 the daughters
60 the tutors
61 garden
62 that is exactly how
63 in possession = in hand, now
64 gold coins★

Let specialities[65] be therefore drawn[66] between us,

That covenants[67] may be kept on either hand.   125

Baptista Ay, when the special thing is well obtained,

That is, her love. For that is all in all.

Petruchio Why that is nothing. For I tell you, father,[68]

I am as peremptory[69] as she proud-minded.

And where two raging fires meet together,   130

They do consume the thing that feeds their fury.

Though little fire grows great with little wind,

Yet extreme gusts will blow out fire and all.

So I to her, and so she yields to me,

For I am rough and woo not like a babe.   135

Baptista Well mayst thou woo, and happy be thy speed.

But be thou armed[70] for some unhappy[71] words.

Petruchio Ay, to the proof, as mountains are for winds,

That[72] shake not though they[73] blow perpetually.

ENTER HORTENSIO, HIS HEAD BROKEN[74]

Baptista How now, my friend, why dost thou look so pale?   140

Hortensio For fear, I promise you, if I look pale.

Baptista What, will my daughter prove a good musician?

---

65 contracts
66 written, drafted, put together
67 agreements, promises
68 marriages created complete family relationships; so too did intended but not
    yet accomplished marriages
69 decisive, conclusive
70 ready
71 mad-tempered, objectionable
72 the mountains that
73 the winds
74 injured

Hortensio I think she'll sooner prove a soldier.[75]

Iron may hold with[76] her, but never lutes.

145 *Baptista*   Why then thou canst not break[77] her to the lute?

Hortensio Why no, for she hath broke the lute to[78] me.

I did but[79] tell her she mistook her frets,[80]

And bowed[81] her hand to teach her fingering,

When (with a most impatient devilish spirit)

150 "Frets, call you these?" quoth she, "I'll fume[82] with them."

And with that word[83] she stroke[84] me on the head,

And through[85] the instrument my pate made way,[86]

And there I stood amazèd[87] for a while,[88]

As on a pillory,[89] looking through the lute,

155 While she did call me rascal, fiddler,[90]

And twangling Jack,[91] with twenty such vile[92] terms,

As she had studied[93] to misuse me so.

75 a total impossibility, then – thus utterly hilarious
76 hold with = endure against
77 train, tame, discipline
78 on
79 only
80 fingering strips
81 bent
82 get angry (as a verb, fret = (1) annoy, (2) destroy)
83 utterance, speech
84 struck
85 right through
86 made way = went ("traveled")
87 stunned, bewildered★
88 moment, short time
89 on a pillory = in stocks: head and hands sticking through, and locked in
90 vagabond
91 twangling Jack = jangling/jingling lout/knave★
92 disgusting, despicable
93 as she had studied = (1) which she employed, (2) as if she had prepared them;
   #1 is more likely

Petruchio Now by the world,[94] it is a lusty[95] wench,

I love[96] her ten times more than e'er I did.

O how I long to have some chat[97] with her. 160

Baptista (*to Hortensio*) Well go with me, and be not so

discomfited.[98]

Proceed in practice with my younger daughter,

She's apt to learn, and thankful for good turns.

Signior Petruchio, will you go with us,

Or shall I send my daughter Kate to you? 165

Petruchio I pray you do.

EXEUNT BAPTISTA, GREMIO, TRANIO, AND HORTENSIO

I will attend[99] her here,

And woo her with some spirit when she comes.

Say that she rail, why then I'll tell her plain[100]

She sings as sweetly as a nightingale.

Say that she frown, I'll say she looks as clear[101] 170

As morning roses newly washed with dew.

Say she be mute, and will not speak a word,

Then I'll commend her volubility,

And say she uttereth piercing[102] eloquence.

---

94 by God, by heaven: more common oaths – but Petruchio swears by the world

95 spirited, lively★

96 Elizabethan love is not identical to romantic love, and is usually much less personal

97 familiar/intimate conversation★

98 dejected, cast down

99 await, wait for

100 flatly, bluntly

101 bright, serene

102 penetrating, keen, sharp

175   If she do bid me pack,[103] I'll give her thanks,

    As though she bid me stay[104] by her a week.

    If she deny[105] to wed, I'll crave[106] the day

    When I shall[107] ask the banns,[108] and when be married.

    But here she comes – and now Petruchio, speak.

ENTER KATE

180   Good morrow Kate, for that's your name, I hear.

Kate   Well have you heard,[109] but something[110] hard of hearing.

    They call me Katherine, that do talk of[111] me.

Petruchio You lie, in faith, for you are called plain Kate,

    And bonny[112] Kate, and sometimes Kate the curst.

185   But Kate, the prettiest Kate in Christendom,

    Kate of Kate Hall, my super-dainty[113] Kate,

    For dainties are all cates,[114] and therefore Kate,

    Take this of me, Kate of my consolation,[115]

    Hearing thy mildness praised in every town,

190   Thy virtues spoke of, and thy beauty sounded,[116]

103 give up, finish
104 remain
105 refuse★
106 ask for, beg to know★
107 must
108 proclamation or other public notice, in church, of intent to marry
109 well have you heard = you have heard well
110 a bit, somewhat
111 about
112 comely, pretty, beautiful★
113 super-dainty = supremely delightful/precious/excellent
114 edible delicacies/dainties
115 comfort, cheering
116 proclaimed, expressed

Yet not so deeply as to thee belongs,

Myself am moved to woo thee for my wife.

Kate   Moved, in good time.[117] Let him that moved you hither

Remove you hence. I knew you at[118] the first,

You were a moveable.[119]

Petruchio   Why, what's[120] a moveable?   195

Kate   A joint-stool.[121]

Petruchio   Thou hast hit[122] it. Come sit on me.[123]

Kate   Asses are made to bear,[124] and so are you.

Petruchio Women are made to bear,[125] and so are you.

Kate   No such jade as bear you, if me you mean.[126]

Petruchio Alas good Kate, I will not burden[127] thee,   200

For knowing[128] thee to be but young and light.[129]

Kate   Too light[130] for such a swain[131] as you to catch,

And yet as heavy[132] as my weight should be.

---

117 in good time = oh really, indeed
118 from
119 furniture ("capable of being moved"; in law, personal as opposed to real property: land)
120 what do you mean
121 a stool made by a professional woodworker (common insult)
122 guessed
123 come sit on me: bawdy invitation to sex
124 carry burdens
125 have children
126 intend, aim at ("have in mind")
127 lie heavy on
128 for knowing = because I know
129 pure ("a virgin")
130 quick, nimble
131 lout, man of insignificant social status★
132 properly weighty (in terms of coins that have been clipped, i.e., lightened of some of their real substance)

Petruchio Should be, should – buzz.[133]

Kate   Well ta'en,[134] and like a
buzzard.[135]

205 *Petruchio* O slow-winged turtle,[136] shall a buzzard take thee?

Kate   Ay, for[137] a turtle, as he[138] takes a buzzard.[139]

Petruchio Come, come, you wasp,[140] i' faith you are too
angry.[141]

Kate   If I be waspish, best beware my sting.

Petruchio My remedy is then to pluck it out.

210 *Kate*   Ay, if the fool could find it where it lies.

Petruchio Who knows not where a wasp does wear his sting?
In his tail.

Kate   In his tongue.[142]

Petruchio   Whose tongue?[143]

Kate   Yours, if you talk of tales,[144] and so farewell.

Petruchio What, with my tongue in your tail? Nay, come
again,[145]

Good Kate, I am a gentleman.

---

133 as a "bee/be" buzzes; rumors – like those about "light" women – were also
said to buzz

134 (1) grasped, captured, (2) understood

135 (1) clumsy, inferior and unteachable hawk, catching the wrong prey,
(2) blockhead, (3) buzzing moth/beetle

136 turtledove

137 mistake me for

138 a turtledove

139 moth, beetle

140 irritable/irascible person

141 sharp, annoying, troublesome

142 telling "tales"

143 not in your "tale" but in your "tail" (genitalia)

144 tails (genitalia)

145 come again = (1) come back (she has started to leave), (2) try once more
("come back to our wordplay")

Kate	That I'll try.[146]	215

SHE STRIKES HIM

Petruchio I swear I'll cuff[147] you if you strike again.

Kate So may you lose your arms.[148]

　　If you strike me, you are no gentleman,

　　And if no gentleman, why then no arms.

Petruchio A herald,[149] Kate? O put me in thy books.　　220

Kate What is your crest,[150] a coxcomb?[151]

Petruchio A combless[152] cock, so[153] Kate will be my hen.

Kate No cock of mine, you crow too like a craven.[154]

Petruchio Nay come Kate, come. You must not look so sour.[155]

Kate It is my fashion when I see a crab.[156]　　225

Petruchio Why, here's no crab, and therefore look not sour.

Kate There is, there is.

Petruchio Then show it me.

Kate Had I[157] a glass[158] I would.

Petruchio What, you mean my face?

Kate Well aimed of such a young
　　one.

146 test
147 (1) slap, (2) put in irons (as, in later usage, in "handcuffs")
148 heraldic coat of arms, signifying gentlemanly status
149 one who maintains the lists/books of those with gentlemanly status
150 symbolic device/figure on coats of arms
151 fools' hat, shaped like a cock's comb
152 removal of a cock's comb: sign of unaggressive/noncombative stance
153 if
154 cock defeated in battle
155 unpleasant, moody, sullen
156 (1) crabapple (very tart), (2) cross/hypercritical person
157 had I = if I had
158 mirror

230 *Petruchio*   Now by Saint George[159] I am too young[160] for you.

     Kate   Yet you are withered.[161]

     Petruchio   'Tis with cares.

     Kate   I care not.

       SHE STARTS TO LEAVE; HE PUTS HIS ARM AROUND HER

     Petruchio   Nay hear you[162] Kate, in sooth, you 'scape not so.

     Kate   I chafe[163] you if I tarry. Let me go.

     Petruchio   No, not a whit, I find you passing gentle.

235   'Twas told me you were rough, and coy, and sullen,

     And now I find report a very liar.

     For thou art pleasant, gamesome,[164] passing courteous,

     But slow[165] in speech. Yet sweet as springtime flowers.

     Thou canst not frown, thou canst not look askance,[166]

240   Nor bite the lip, as angry wenches will,

     Nor hast thou pleasure to be cross[167] in talk.

     But thou with mildness entertain'st[168] thy wooers,

     With gentle conference,[169] soft, and affable.

     Why does the world report that Kate doth limp?

245   O sland'rous world. Kate like the hazel-twig

     Is straight, and slender, and as brown in hue

---

159 English soldier-hero
160 in youthful/vigorous condition
161 (1) wrinkled, (2) wasted, shriveled
162 pay attention
163 (1) gall, irritate, (2) excite, inflame
164 playful, merry
165 dull
166 sideways (with suspicion, disdain)
167 contrary, perverse, quarrelsome
168 deal with, treat, receive
169 conversation, talk

As hazel-nuts, and sweeter than the kernels.

HE RELEASES HER

O let me see thee walk. Thou dost not halt.[170]

Kate   Go fool, and whom thou keep'st command.[171]

Petruchio Did ever Dian[172] so become[173] a grove   250
    As Kate this chamber with her princely[174] gait?
    O be thou Dian, and let her be Kate,
    And then let Kate be chaste,[175] and Dian sportful.[176]

Kate   Where did you study all this goodly speech?

Petruchio It is extempore,[177] from my mother-wit.[178]   255

Kate   A witty mother, witless else her son.[179]

Petruchio Am I not wise?

Kate   Yes, keep you warm.[180]

Petruchio Marry, so I mean sweet Katherine, in thy bed.
    And therefore setting all this chat aside,
    Thus in plain terms. Your father hath consented   260
    That you shall be my wife. Your dowry 'greed[181] on,
    And will you, nill you,[182] I will marry you.

170 limp★
171 whom thou keep'st command = give orders to those you employ ("pay to serve you")
172 Diana, goddess of hunting, of open country and forests
173 grace, suit
174 regal, royal
175 (1) reserved, restrained, (2) virginal, as Diana was
176 lively, frolicsome
177 offhand, without preparation
178 natural intelligence
179 else her son = otherwise would her son be totally devoid of brains
180 proverbial: "He is wise enough who can keep himself warm"
181 is agreed
182 whether you want to, whether you don't want to ("willy-nilly")

Now Kate, I am a husband for your turn,
For by this light, whereby I see thy beauty,
265 Thy beauty that doth make me like thee well,
Thou must be married to no man but me,
For I am he am born to tame you, Kate,
And bring you from a wild Kate to a Kate
Conformable as[183] other household[184] Kates.
270 Here comes your father. Never make denial,
I must and will have Katherine to my wife.

ENTER BAPTISTA, GREMIO, AND TRANIO

Baptista Now Signior Petruchio, how speed you with my
daughter?

Petruchio How but well sir? How but well?
It were impossible I should speed amiss.

275 *Baptista* Why how now daughter Katherine? In your
dumps?[185]

Kate   Call you me daughter? Now I promise you
You have showed a tender fatherly regard,
To wish me wed to one half lunatic,
A madcap ruffian,[186] and a swearing Jack,
280 That thinks with oaths to face[187] the matter out.

Petruchio Father, 'tis thus, yourself and all the world
That talked of her have talked amiss of her.
If she be curst, it is for policy,[188]
For she's not froward, but modest as the dove,

---

183 (1) similar to, harmonious with, (2) compliant/submissive
184 domestic
185 having no liveliness (like dumpling dough)
186 madcap ruffian = crazy/reckless/wildly impulsive brute/criminal
187 bluff*
188 prudence, artfulness, sagacity

	She is not hot,[189] but temperate as the morn,	285
	For patience she will prove a second Grissel,[190]	
	And Roman Lucrece[191] for her chastity.	
	And to conclude, we have 'greed so well together	
	That upon Sunday is the wedding day.	
Kate	I'll see thee hanged on Sunday first.	290
Gremio	Hark Petruchio, she says she'll see thee hanged first.	
Tranio	Is this your speeding? Nay then goodnight our part![192]	
Petruchio	Be patient gentlemen, I choose her for myself,	
	If she and I be pleased, what's that to you?	
	'Tis bargained[193] 'twixt us twain being[194] alone,	295
	That she shall still be curst in company.	
	I tell you 'tis incredible to believe	
	How much she loves me. O the kindest Kate,	
	She hung about my neck, and kiss on kiss	
	She vied[195] so fast, protesting[196] oath on oath,	300
	That in a twink[197] she won me to her love.	
	O you are novices, 'tis a world[198] to see	
	How tame, when men and women are alone,	
	A meacock wretch[199] can make the curstest shrew.	

189 ardent, quick-tempered
190 patient Griselda: legendary wife submissive in everything (griZELL)
191 Lucretia so valued sexual purity that, having been raped, she committed
   suicide (here, LOOkrees)
192 share, portion
193 agreed
194 when we were
195 piled up, displayed
196 declaring
197 twinkling
198 delight, marvel
199 meacock wretch = weakling/cowardly hapless/contemptible/despicable
   man

305 Give me thy hand Kate, I will[200] unto Venice

To buy apparel 'gainst[201] the wedding day.

Provide the feast[202] father, and bid[203] the guests:

I will be sure my Katherine shall be fine.[204]

Baptista   I know not what to say; but give me your hands.

310 God send you joy, Petruchio, 'tis a match.[205]

Gremio, Tranio   Amen, say we, we will be witnesses.

Petruchio   Father, and wife, and gentlemen adieu.

I will to Venice, Sunday comes apace,[206]

We will have rings and things, and fine array,

315 And kiss me Kate, we will be married a' Sunday.

EXEUNT PETRUCHIO AND KATE

Gremio   Was ever match clapped up[207] so suddenly?

Baptista   Faith gentlemen, now I play a merchant's part,

And venture madly[208] on a desperate mart.[209]

Tranio   'Twas a commodity[210] lay fretting[211] by[212] you,

320 'Twill bring you gain, or perish on the seas.

Baptista   The gain I seek is, quiet in[213] the match.

---

200 will go
201 for, in anticipation of
202 celebration*
203 invite
204 perfect, exquisite, admirable, beautiful
205 settled marital alliance
206 swiftly
207 clapped up = agreed upon: reciprocal hand-clapping signaled a settled bargain
208 venture madly = dare/risk foolishly/insanely
209 desperate mart = dangerous market (a daughter's marriage)
210 salable object
211 (1) wasting, (2) impatient
212 nearby
213 Folio: me; all editors emend

Gremio No doubt but he hath got a quiet[214] catch.

    But now Baptista, to your younger daughter:

    Now is the day we long have looked for.

    I am your neighbor, and was suitor first.   325

Tranio   And I am one that love Bianca more

    Than words can witness, or your thoughts can guess.

Gremio Youngling, thou canst not love so dear[215] as I.

Tranio   Greybeard, thy love doth freeze.[216]

Gremio   But thine doth fry.[217]

    Skipper,[218] stand back, 'tis age that nourisheth.   330

Tranio   But youth in ladies' eyes that flourisheth.[219]

Baptista Content you gentlemen, I will compound this strife.

    'Tis deeds must win the prize, and he of both[220]

    That can assure my daughter greatest dower,

    Shall have my Bianca's love.   335

    Say Signior Gremio, what can you assure her?[221]

Gremio First, as you know, my house within the city

    Is richly furnishèd with plate[222] and gold,

    Basins and ewers to lave[223] her dainty hands.

    My hangings[224] all of Tyrian[225] tapestry.   340

---

214 peaceful
215 (1) lovingly, tenderly, (2) expensively
216 chill a woman
217 scorch
218 irresponsible young person
219 thrives, blossoms
220 the two of you
221 by jointure, to be hers if she survives her husband
222 silver utensils
223 wash, bathe
224 wall hangings (drapes, curtains, tapestries)
225 Middle Eastern commercial center, originally Phoenician

In ivory coffers[226] I have stuffed my crowns,
In cypress chests my arras counterpoints,[227]
Costly apparel, tents,[228] and canopies,[229]
Fine linen, Turkey cushions bossed[230] with pearl,
345   Valance[231] of Venice gold[232] in needle-work,
Pewter[233] and brass, and all things that belong
To house or housekeeping. Then at my farm
I have a hundred milch-kine[234] to the pail,[235]
Six score[236] fat oxen standing in my stalls,[237]
350   And all things answerable to this portion.[238]
Myself am struck in years,[239] I must confess,
And if I die tomorrow this is hers,
If whilst I live she will be only mine.

Tranio That "only" came well in. Sir, list to me,
355   I am my father's heir and only son.
If I may have your daughter to my wife,
I'll leave her houses three or four as good
Within rich Pisa's walls, as any one
Old Signior Gremio has in Padua,

226 boxes, chests
227 arras counterpoints = tapestry counterpanes/quilts (woven in Arras, city in
    N France)
228 bed hangings/curtains
229 overhanging covers for beds
230 embossed
231 short curtain/border
232 gold thread
233 utensils of a lead and tin alloy
234 milk cows
235 to the pail = being milked for sale
236 score = 20
237 separated sections in a barn/shed
238 answerable to this portion = suitable/corresponding to this dowry
239 advanced in years ("stricken")

Besides, two thousand ducats by the year[240]   360
Of fruitful land, all which shall be her jointure.
What, have I pinched[241] you, Signior Gremio?

Gremio   (*aside*) Two thousand ducats by the year of land?
My land amounts not to so much in all. –
That[242] she shall have, besides an argosy[243]   365
That now is lying in Marseilles' road.[244]
What, have I choked you with an argosy?

Tranio   Gremio, 'tis known my father hath no less
Than three great argosies, besides two galliasses,[245]
And twelve tight galleys,[246] these I will assure her,   370
And twice as much, whate'er thou offer'st next.

Gremio   Nay, I have offered all, I have no more,
And she can have no more than all I have.
If you like me,[247] she shall have me and mine.

Tranio   Why, then the maid is mine from[248] all the world   375
By your firm promise, Gremio is out-vied.[249]

Baptista   I must confess your offer is the best,
And let your father make her the assurance,[250]
She is your own, else you must pardon me.

---

240 rented out by the year
241 squeezed, strained, afflicted
242 all of this
243 very large merchant ship
244 anchoring place ("roadstead")
245 heavy, low-built galley-type ship, larger than a normal galley
246 tight galleys = watertight low, flat, one-deck ships, employing both sail and
    oarsmen
247 if you like me = if I please you, Baptista
248 against, away from ("in competition with")
249 outbid
250 documents guaranteeing the jointure

380   If you should die before him, where's her dower?[251]

    Tranio   That's but a cavil.[252] He is old, I young.

    Gremio   And may not young men die as well as old?

    Baptista   Well gentlemen,

    I am thus resolved. On Sunday next, you know

385   My daughter Katherine is to be married.

    Now on the Sunday following, shall Bianca

    Be bride to you,[253] if you make this assurance.

    If not, to Signior Gremio.

    And so I take my leave, and thank you both.

    Gremio   Adieu, good neighbor.

EXIT BAPTISTA

390   Now I fear thee not.

    Sirrah, young gamester,[254] your father were a fool

    To give thee all, and in his waning age

    Set foot under thy table.[255] Tut, a toy,[256]

    An old Italian fox is not so kind,[257] my boy.

EXIT GREMIO

395 *Tranio*   A vengeance[258] on your crafty withered hide!

    Yet I have faced it with a card of ten.[259]

    'Tis in my head to do my master good.

251 not "dowry," but "jointure"
252 quibble
253 Tranio/Lucentio
254 gambler
255 set foot under thy table = have to live in your house/be dependent on you
256 foolish joke, fantasy, weird notion
257 generous, benevolent
258 a vengeance = curses
259 faced it with a card of ten = put on a bold front with a ten-card

I see no reason but[260] supposed Lucentio
Must get a father, called "supposed Vincentio,"
And that's a wonder.[261] Fathers commonly   400
Do get[262] their children. But in this case of wooing
A child shall get a sire, if I fail not of my cunning.

EXIT

---

260 reason but = logical supposition / premise except that
261 astonishment, surprise★
262 beget, engender

Act 3

SCENE I

Baptista's house

ENTER LUCENTIO, HORTENSIO, AND BIANCA

Lucentio   Fiddler forbear,[1] you grow too forward, sir.
  Have you so soon forgot the entertainment
  Her sister Katherine welcomed you withal?
Hortensio But wrangling pedant,[2] this[3] is
5   The patroness of heavenly harmony.[4]
  Then give me leave to have prerogative,[5]
  And when in music we have spent an hour,
  Your lecture[6] shall have leisure[7] for as much.
Lucentio   Preposterous[8] ass, that never read so far

---

1 refrain, control yourself
2 (1) quarrelsome academic/bookworm, (2) schoolmaster
3 Bianca
4 (1) peace, concord, (2) pleasing/melodious sounds
5 prior rights
6 reading and explicating aloud
7 opportunity, freedom
8 perverse, irrational ("backwards-thinking")

To[9] know the cause why music was ordained.[10]   10
Was it not to refresh the mind of man
After his studies, or his usual[11] pain?
Then give me leave to read philosophy,
And while[12] I pause, serve in[13] your harmony.

Hortensio Sirrah, I will not bear these braves[14] of thine.   15

Bianca   Why gentlemen, you do me double wrong,
To strive for that which resteth in my choice.
I am no breeching[15] scholar in the schools,
I'll not be tied to hours, nor 'pointed[16] times,
But learn my lessons as I please myself.   20
And to cut off all strife, here sit we down,
Take you your instrument, play you the whiles,[17]
His lecture will be done ere you have tuned.

Hortensio You'll leave his lecture when I am in tune?

Lucentio   That will be never, tune your instrument.   25

Bianca   Where left we last?

Lucentio   Here madam:[18]

Hic ibat Simois, hic est Sigeia tellus,
Hic steterat Priami regia celsa senis.[19]

9 so as to
10 established, founded ("created")
11 common, habitual
12 when
13 up
14 bravados, swaggering, challenges★
15 novice
16 fixed ("appointed")
17 during that time
18 my lady★ (French: ma dame)
19 "Here the Simois flowed, here is the Trojan plain, here stood old Priam's
   towering palace" (Ovid *Heroides* ["Letters from Heroines"] 1.33–34)

30 *Bianca*   Construe them.[20]

Lucentio   "Hic ibat," as I told you before, "Simois," I am
           Lucentio, "hic est," son unto[21] Vincentio of Pisa, "Sigeia
           tellus," disguised thus to get your love, "Hic steterat," and that
           Lucentio that comes a-wooing, "Priami," is my man Tranio,
35   "regia," bearing my port, "celsa senis," that we might beguile
           the old pantaloon.[22]

Hortensio Madam, my instrument's in tune.

Bianca   Let's hear.

HORTENSIO PLAYS

O fie, the treble jars.[23]

Lucentio   Spit in the hole,[24] man, and tune again.

40 *Bianca*   Now let me see if I can construe it: "Hic ibat Simois,"
           I know you not, "hic est Sigeia tellus," I trust you not, "Hic
           steterat Priami," take heed he hear us not, "regia," presume
           not, "celsa senis," despair not.

Hortensio Madam, 'tis now in tune.

Lucentio   All but the bass.

45 *Hortensio* The bass is right, 'tis the base knave that jars.[25]

           (*aside*) How fiery and forward our pedant is.

           Now for my life the knave doth court[26] my love.

           Pedascule,[27] I'll watch you better yet.

---

20 construe them = grammatically analyze the lines
21 of
22 foolish / clownlike man: Gremio
23 clashes, makes a discordant sound★
24 spit in the hole = (1) moisten the tuning peg by spitting on it, so it can be
   adjusted more easily (?), (2) spit on your hands and get it done (?)
25 the Folio assigns the next three lines to Lucentio; all editors emend
26 doth court = actually is courting
27 little pedant

Bianca   (*to Lucentio*) In time I may believe, yet I mistrust.[28]

Lucentio   Mistrust it not. For sure, Aeacides[29]   50

    Was Ajax, called so from[30] his grandfather.

Bianca   I must believe my master,[31] else I promise you,

    I should be arguing still upon that doubt,

    But let it rest. Now, Litio, to you.

    Good master, take it not unkindly pray   55

    That I have been thus pleasant[32] with you both.

Hortensio (*to Lucentio*) You may go walk and give me leave[33] awhile,

    My lessons make no music in three parts.

Lucentio   Are you so formal, sir? (*aside*) Well I must wait

    And watch withal, for but I be deceived,   60

    Our fine musician groweth amorous.

Hortensio Madam, before you touch the instrument,

    To learn the order of my fingering

    I must begin with rudiments of art,

    To teach you gamut[34] in a briefer sort,   65

    More pleasant, pithy, and effectual[35]

    Than hath been taught by any of my trade,[36]

    And there it is in writing, fairly drawn.[37]

Bianca   Why, I am past my gamut long ago.

---

28 the Folio assigns this line to Hortensio; all editors emend
29 eyASSiDEEZ
30 after
31 schoolmaster, teacher
32 jocular, facetious, merry
33 permission, opportunity
34 the scale
35 pithy, and effectual = vigorous/solid and effective/efficient
36 profession
37 fairly drawn = neatly/elegantly delineated/written

70 *Hortensio* Yet read the gamut of Hortensio.

   Bianca   (*reading*) "Gamut I am, the ground of all accord,[38]

      A *re,* to plead Hortensio's passion,

      B *mi,* Bianca, take him for thy lord,

      C *fa ut,* that loves with all affection,

75   D *sol re,* one clef, two notes have I,

      E *la mi,* show pity or I die."

      Call you this gamut? Tut, I like it not.

      Old fashions please me best, I am not so nice[39]

      To charge true rules[40] for old inventions.[41]

ENTER SERVANT

80 *Servant*   Mistress, your father prays you leave your books,

      And help to dress your sister's chamber up,[42]

      You know tomorrow is the wedding day.

   Bianca   Farewell sweet masters both, I must be gone.

EXEUNT BIANCA AND SERVANT

   Lucentio   Faith mistress, then I have no cause to stay.

EXIT LUCENTIO

85 *Hortensio* But I have cause to pry into this pedant.

      Methinks he looks as though he were in love.

      Yet if thy thoughts, Bianca, be so humble[43]

---

38 ground of all accord = basis / essence of all harmony
39 fussy, fastidious
40 charge true rules = overload / burden the constant / reliable / certain rules
41 methods
42 dress . . . up = (1) straighten, prepare, ready, (2) adorn, array
43 lowly (negative sense)

To cast thy wand'ring[44] eyes on every stale,[45]
Seize thee that list:[46] if once I find thee ranging,[47]
Hortensio will be quit with[48] thee by changing.[49]   90

EXIT

44 vagrant, roaming
45 decoy, lying in ambush
46 seize thee that list = take / capture whoever you like
47 roaming, wandering, straying
48 quit with = rid of
49 substituting someone else in your place

SCENE 2

In front of Baptista's house

ENTER BAPTISTA, GREMIO, TRANIO, KATE, BIANCA,
LUCENTIO, AND ATTENDANTS

Baptista Signior Lucentio, this is the 'pointed day
That Katherine and Petruchio should be married,
And yet we hear not of our son-in-law.
What will be said, what mockery[1] will it be?
5   To want the bridegroom when the priest attends[2]
To speak the ceremonial rites of marriage?
What says Lucentio to this shame of ours?

Kate   No shame but mine, I must forsooth be forced
To give my hand, opposed against my heart,
10   Unto a mad-brain rudesby,[3] full of spleen,[4]
Who wooed in haste, and means to wed at leisure.
I told you, I, he was a frantic[5] fool,
Hiding his bitter jests in blunt behavior,
And to be noted for a merry man.
15   He'll woo a thousand, 'point the day of marriage,
Make friends invited, and proclaim the banns,
Yet never means to wed where he hath wooed.
Now must the world point at poor Katherine,
And say, lo, there is mad Petruchio's wife –
20   If it would please him come and marry her.

1 subject of ridicule / derision
2 is / will be present
3 insolent / unmannerly / disorderly fellow
4 whims, caprices
5 lunatic

Tranio   Patience good Katherine, and Baptista too.
   Upon my life, Petruchio means but well,
   Whatever fortune stays[6] him from his word.
   Though he be blunt, I know him[7] passing wise.
   Though he be merry, yet withal he's honest.[8]   25
Kate   Would Katherine had never seen him though.

   EXIT KATE, WEEPING, FOLLOWED BY BIANCA
   AND ATTENDANTS

Baptista Go girl, I cannot blame thee now to weep,
   For such an injury[9] would vex a very saint,
   Much more a shrew of thy impatient humor.

   ENTER BIONDELLO

Biondello Master, master, news, news, and such old[10] news as you   30
   never heard of!
Baptista   Is it new and old too? How may that be?
Biondello Why, is it not news to hear of Petruchio's coming?
Baptista   Is he come?
Biondello Why no sir.   35
Baptista   What then?
Biondello He is coming.
Baptista   When will he be here?
Biondello When he stands where I am, and sees you there.

6 stops, keeps
7 him to be
8 honorable, decent, respectable★
9 insult
10 grand, abundant (not in the Folio; most editors emend, because of Baptista's
   following query)

40 *Tranio* But say,[11] what to[12] thine old news?

Biondello Why, Petruchio is coming, in a new hat and an old
jerkin,[13] a pair of old breeches[14] thrice turned,[15] a pair of
boots that have been candle-cases,[16] one buckled, another
laced, an old rusty sword ta'en out of the town armory,[17] with

45 a broken hilt, and chapeless,[18] with two broken points.[19] His
horse hipped,[20] with an old mothy saddle, and stirrups of no
kindred,[21] besides possessed[22] with the glanders[23] and like to[24]
mose in the chine,[25] troubled with the lampas,[26] infected with
the fashions,[27] full of windgalls,[28] sped with spavins,[29] rayed

50 with the yellows,[30] past cure of the fives,[31] stark spoiled with

11 speak, tell us

12 what to = what about/of

13 close-fitting jacket/short coat

14 trousers that reach to just below the knee

15 altered

16 old, worn-out boots that had been relegated to use as storage boxes for
candles

17 town armory = town/local/common arsenal

18 unsheathed

19 straps

20 lame in the hips

21 of no kindred = not resembling each other

22 affected

23 contagious equine disease

24 likely★

25 mose in the chine = (?) suffer/ache in the spine/back

26 equine disease: swelling of the roof of the mouth

27 farcy: infectious equine disease

28 equine leg tumors

29 sped with spavins = sick/brought down/finished★ by cartilage inflammation
in a horse's leg

30 rayed with the yellows = berayed/disfigured/defiled★ by equine/bovine
jaundice

31 avives (aVIVES): equine glandular swelling

the staggers,[32] begnawn[33] with the bots,[34] swayed in the
back, and shoulder-shotten,[35] near-legged before,[36] and with
a half-checked[37] bit, and a head-stall[38] of sheep's leather,[39]
which being restrained[40] to keep him from stumbling, hath
been often burst, and now repaired with knots.[41] One girth[42]   55
six times pieced,[43] and a woman's crupper[44] of velure,[45]
which hath two letters for her[46] name, fairly set down in
studs,[47] and here and there pieced with pack-thread.[48]

Baptista   Who comes with him?

Biondello   O sir, his lackey,[49] for all the world caparisoned[50] like   60
the horse. With a linen stock[51] on one leg, and a kersey boot-
hose[52] on the other, gartered with a red and blue list,[53] an old

32 stark spoiled with the staggers = severely ravaged by an equine illness like
   "mad cow disease"
33 corroded
34 parasitical maggots/worms
35 shoulder-ruined ("shot")
36 front legs coming too close to one another (knock-kneed?)
37 half-loose
38 part of bridle/halter going around the horse's head
39 inferior (pigskin was favored by men of social standing)
40 tightened
41 knotted leather (cheap, poverty-stricken appearance)
42 leather band around horse's belly, securing saddle/pack on its back
43 patched, mended
44 strap running from back of saddle to the horse's tail and then around under
   the horse, to hold saddle from sliding forward; not generally used by men★
45 velvet
46 the prior owner's
47 set down in studs = mounted/written out by metal nails
48 twine, heavy thread
49 footman, valet
50 wearing trappings/decorated
51 stocking
52 kersey boot-hose = coarse woolen long overstocking
53 cloth strip/border

hat, and the "humor of forty fancies"[54] pricked in't for[55] a
feather. A monster, a very monster in apparel, and not like a
Christian footboy, or a gentleman's lackey.

65

Tranio   'Tis some odd humor pricks[56] him to this fashion,
Yet oftentimes he goes but mean-appareled.[57]

Baptista   I am glad he's come, howsoe'er he comes.

Biondello   Why sir, he comes not.

70 Baptista   Didst thou not say he comes?

Biondello   Who, that Petruchio came?

Baptista   Ay, that Petruchio came.

Biondello   No sir, I say his horse comes with him on his back.

Baptista   Why that's all one.

75 Biondello   Nay by Saint Jamy,

I hold[58] you a penny,

A horse and a man

Is more than one,

And yet not many.[59]

ENTER PETRUCHIO AND GRUMIO

80 Petruchio   Come, where be these gallants?[60] Who's at home?

Baptista   You are welcome sir.

Petruchio   And yet I come not well.[61]

---

54 reference unknown; perhaps the name of a set of lost ballads (printed on
  broadside sheets and thus ephemeral)

55 pricked in't for = pinned on to the hat instead of a feather

56 drives, urges, incites

57 wearing poor/low-class clothing

58 bet

59 origin unknown

60 fine/finely dressed gentlemen*

61 come not well = do not arrive satisfactorily/like someone in good favor/
  welcome

Baptista   And yet you halt[62] not.

Tranio   Not so well appareled
   As I wish you were.

Petruchio   Were it better,[63] I should rush in thus.
   But where is Kate? Where is my lovely bride?   85
   How does my father? Gentles, methinks you frown,
   And wherefore gaze this goodly company,
   As if they saw some wondrous monument,[64]
   Some comet or unusual prodigy?[65]

Baptista   Why, sir, you know this is your wedding day.   90
   First were we sad, fearing you would not come,
   Now sadder, that you come so unprovided.[66]
   Fie, doff this habit,[67] shame[68] to your estate,[69]
   An eyesore to our solemn festival.[70]

Tranio   And tell us what occasion of import[71]   95
   Hath all[72] so long detained you from your wife,
   And sent you hither so unlike yourself?

Petruchio   Tedious it were to tell, and harsh[73] to hear,
   Sufficeth I am come to keep my word,

62 Baptista avoids Petruchio's question by taking "come" in the sense of "move,
   walk"
63 even were my clothing better
64 sign, token, portent
65 (1) omen, (2) marvel, abnormal/monstrous thing
66 unequipped, unready
67 doff this habit = take off this clothing★
68 a shame
69 condition, social standing
70 solemn festival = dignified/sanctified celebration
71 significance (imPORT)
72 completely, entirely
73 disagreeable, jarring, offensive★

100   Though in some part enforced to digress,[74]

       Which at more leisure I will so excuse

       As you shall well be satisfied withal.

       But where is Kate? I stay[75] too long from her,

       The morning wears,[76] 'tis time we were at church.

105 *Tranio*   See not your bride in these unreverent robes.

       Go to my chamber, put on clothes of mine.

    Petruchio Not I, believe me, thus I'll visit her.

    Baptista   But thus I trust you will not marry her.

    Petruchio Good sooth[77] even thus, therefore ha' done with

       words,

110   To me she's married, not unto my clothes.

       Could I repair[78] what she will wear in me,

       As I can change these poor accoutrements,[79]

       'Twere well for Kate and better for myself.

       But what a fool am I to chat with you,

115   When I should bid good morrow to my bride,

       And seal the title with a lovely kiss.

      EXEUNT PETRUCHIO, GRUMIO, AND BIODELLO

Tranio   He hath some meaning[80] in his mad attire.

       We will persuade him, be it possible,

       To put on better ere he go to church.

---

74 enforced to digress = obliged to deviate
75 remain
76 is getting on / wasting away* (possibly a bawdy reference to wearing horns, i.e., being cuckolded)
77 good sooth = truly
78 set in order, heal, renew
79 garments
80 intention, purpose

Baptista   I'll after him and see the event[81] of this.   120

    EXEUNT BAPTISTA, GREMIO, AND ATTENDANTS

Tranio   (*to Lucentio*) But sir, love concerneth us[82] to add[83]
    Her father's liking,[84] which to bring to pass
    As I before imparted to your worship,
    I am to get a man – whate'er he be
    It skills not much,[85] we'll fit[86] him to our turn –   125
    And he shall be Vincentio of Pisa,
    And make assurance[87] here in Padua
    Of greater sums than I have promisèd,
    So shall you quietly enjoy your hope,[88]
    And marry sweet Bianca with consent.   130
Lucentio   Were it not that my fellow schoolmaster
    Doth watch Bianca's steps so narrowly,[89]
    'Twere good methinks to steal[90] our marriage,
    Which once performed, let all the world say no,
    I'll keep mine own despite[91] of all the world.   135
Tranio   That by degrees[92] we[93] mean to look into,

81 outcome, result
82 concerneth us = obliges you and me
83 speak further about
84 approval, consent – which is conditional upon formal financial guarantees
85 skills not much = makes no difference, does not matter
86 adapt
87 guarantee, at some point put into writing
88 enjoy your hope = have/possess your desire
89 carefully
90 secretly perform
91 in spite
92 by degrees = little by little, gradually
93 (?) has Tranio fallen into the aristocratic/royal "we"? The sixth line of this
   speech suggests that he has

And watch our vantage[94] in this business.
We'll overreach[95] the greybeard, Gremio,
The narrow-prying father, Minóla,
140   The quaint[96] musician, amorous Litio –
All for my master's sake, Lucentio.

ENTER GREMIO

Signior Gremio, came you from the church?
Gremio As willingly as e'er I came from school.
Tranio And is the bride and bridegroom coming home?
145 *Gremio* A bridegroom say you? 'Tis a groom[97] indeed,
A grumbling groom, and that the girl shall find.
Tranio Curster than she? Why, 'tis impossible.
Gremio Why, he's a devil, a devil, a very fiend.
Tranio Why, she's a devil, a devil, the devil's dam.
150 *Gremio* Tut, she's a lamb, a dove, a fool, to[98] him.
I'll tell you Sir Lucentio, when the priest
Should[99] ask if Katherine should be his wife,
"Ay, by gogs-wouns"[100] quoth he, and swore so loud
That all amazed the priest let fall the book,
155.   And as he stooped again to take[101] it up,
The mad-brained bridegroom took him such a cuff[102]
That down fell priest and book, and book and priest.

94 opportunity, chances
95 outdo, get the better of
96 ingenious, clever, cunning
97 stable hand
98 compared to
99 was required to
100 by gogs-wouns = by God's wounds, a vulgar oath
101 pick
102 took him such a cuff = gave him such a smack/blow

"Now take them up," quoth he, "if any list."

Tranio   What said the wench when he[103] rose again?

Gremio   Trembled and shook. For why, he[104] stamped and swore,   160
As if the vicar meant to cozen[105] him.
But after many ceremonies[106] done,
He calls for wine. "A health," quoth he, as if
He had been aboard carousing to his mates
After a storm, quaffed off the muscadel,[107]   165
And threw the sops[108] all in the sexton's face,
Having no other reason
But that his beard grew thin and hungerly[109]
And seemed[110] to ask him[111] sops as he[112] was drinking.
This done, he took the bride about[113] the neck,   170
And kissed her lips with such a clamorous smack,
That at the parting[114] all the church did echo.
And I seeing this came thence for very shame,
And after me I know the rout[115] is coming.
Such a mad marriage never was before.   175
Hark, hark, I hear the minstrels play.

---

103 the priest
104 Petruchio
105 cheat, defraud★
106 religious rites
107 sweet wine, which should then have been shared by the bride and the
    guests ("muscatel")
108 bits of cake placed in the wine
109 sparsely, hungrily
110 (?) he, the sexton, appeared
111 him for the
112 Petruchio
113 took … about = grasped/lay hold of … around
114 taking away of his lips
115 company, crowd

MUSIC

ENTER PETRUCHIO, KATE, BIANCA, BAPTISTA,
HORTENSIO, GRUMIO, AND OTHERS

Petruchio Gentlemen and friends, I thank you for your pains.
I know you think to dine with me today,
And have prepared great store of wedding cheer,
180 But so it is, my haste doth call me hence,
And therefore here I mean to take my leave.
Baptista Is't possible you will[116] away tonight?
Petruchio I must away today before night come.
Make it no wonder.[117] If you knew my business,
185 You would entreat me rather go than stay.
And honest company, I thank you all,
That have beheld me give away myself
To this most patient, sweet, and virtuous wife.
Dine with my father, drink a health to me,
190 For I must hence, and farewell to you all.
Tranio Let us entreat you stay till after dinner.
Petruchio It may not be.
Gremio   Let me entreat you.
Petruchio It cannot be.
Kate   Let me entreat you.
Petruchio I am content.
Kate   Are you content to stay?
195 *Petruchio* I am content you shall entreat me stay,
But yet not stay, entreat me how you can.
Kate   Now if you love me, stay.

116 are going
117 make it no wonder = don't be astonished

94

Petruchio	Grumio, my horse.[118]
Grumio	Ay sir, they be ready, the oats have eaten the horses.
Kate	Nay then,

Do[119] what thou canst, I will not go today;   200

No, nor tomorrow, not till I please myself.

The door is open sir, there lies your way,

You may be[120] jogging whiles your boots are green.[121]

For me, I'll not be gone till I please myself,

'Tis like you'll prove a jolly[122] surly groom,   205

That take it on you at the first so roundly.

Petruchio O Kate content thee, prithee be not angry.

Kate   I will be angry, what hast thou to do?

Father, be quiet, he shall stay[123] my leisure.

Gremio   Ay marry sir, now it begins to work.[124]   210

Kate   Gentlemen, forward to the bridal dinner.

I see a woman may be made a fool

If she had not a spirit to resist.

Petruchio They shall go forward Kate, at thy command.

Obey the bride, you that attend on her,   215

Go to the feast, revel and domineer,[125]

Carouse full measure[126] to her maidenhead,[127]

Be mad and merry, or go hang yourselves.

118 horses
119 you do
120 may be = are allowed to be
121 still new/clean
122 arrogant, overbearing
123 await
124 happen ("here we go")
125 revel and domineer = make merry★ and roister/feast riotously
126 carouse full measure = drink freely
127 her virginity, about to be lost

But for my bonny Kate, she must[128] with me.
220 (*to Kate*) Nay, look not big,[129] nor stamp, nor stare, nor fret,
I will be master of what is mine own.
She is my goods, my chattels,[130] she is my house,
My household stuff,[131] my field, my barn,
My horse, my ox, my ass, my anything,
225 And here she stands, touch her whoever dare,
I'll bring mine action[132] on the proudest he[133]
That stops my way in Padua. Grumio,
Draw forth thy weapon, we are beset[134] with thieves,
Rescue thy mistress, if thou be a man.
230 (*to Kate*) Fear not sweet wench, they shall not touch thee, Kate,
I'll buckler[135] thee against a million.

EXEUNT PETRUCHIO, KATE, AND GRUMIO

Baptista Nay, let them go, a couple of quiet ones.
Gremio Went they not quickly, I should die with laughing.
Tranio Of all mad matches never was the like.
235 *Lucentio* Mistress, what's your opinion of your sister?
Bianca That being mad herself, she's madly mated.
Gremio I warrant him[136] Petruchio is Kated.
Baptista Neighbors and friends, though bride and bridegroom
wants[137]

128 must go
129 mighty, important, haughty
130 moveable property
131 stores
132 (1) fight, (2) legal action
133 man
134 surrounded by
135 shield, defend, protect
136 I warrant him = I guarantee/promise
137 are lacking

For to supply the places at the table,
You know there wants no junkets[138] at the feast.   240
Lucentio, you shall supply the bridegroom's place,
And let Bianca take her sister's room.[139]

Tranio   Shall sweet Bianca practice how to bride it?
Baptista   She shall Lucentio. Come gentlemen, let's go.

EXEUNT

138 delicacies
139 place

Act 4

𝕲

Petruchio's country house

ENTER GRUMIO

Grumio Fie, fie on all tired jades, on all mad masters, and all foul
ways! Was ever man so beaten?[1] Was ever man so rayed?[2]
Was ever man so weary? I am sent before[3] to make a fire, and
they are coming after to warm them. Now, were not I a little
pot,[4] and soon hot,[5] my very lips might freeze to my teeth,
my tongue to the roof of my mouth, my heart in my belly, ere
I should come by a fire to thaw me, but I with blowing the
fire shall warm myself. For considering the weather, a taller
man than I will take cold. Holla, ho Curtis!

ENTER CURTIS

1 (1) struck, (2) worked hard
2 striped with mud
3 ahead
4 little pot = short person
5 proverbial: a small pot boils faster

98

Curtis Who is that calls so coldly?[6] 10

Grumio A piece of ice. If thou doubt it, thou mayst slide from my shoulder to my heel, with no greater[7] a run but[8] my head and my neck. A fire, good Curtis.

Curtis Is my master and his wife coming, Grumio?

Grumio O ay Curtis, ay, and therefore fire, fire, cast on no 15
water.[9]

Curtis Is she so hot a shrew as she's reported?

Grumio She was, good Curtis, before this frost. But thou knowest winter tames man, woman, and beast. For it hath tamed my old[10] master, and my new[11] mistress, and myself, 20
fellow[12] Curtis.

Curtis Away, you three-inch fool, I am no beast.[13]

Grumio Am I but three inches? Why, thy horn[14] is a foot, and so long am I[15] at the least. But wilt thou make a fire, or shall I complain on thee to our mistress, whose hand, she being now 25
at hand,[16] thou shalt soon feel, to thy cold comfort,[17] for being slow in thy hot office?

Curtis I prithee good Grumio, tell me, how goes the world?

Grumio A cold world, Curtis, in every office but thine, and

6 uncordially
7 bigger
8 except for
9 a then very popular song contained the line "cast on water"
10 existing
11 brand new
12 comrade, co-worker★
13 mere animal (the opposite of a man)
14 penis
15 long am I = (1) tall am I, (2) long is my penis
16 at hand = close by, near
17 cold comfort = uncordial/unhappy pleasure/consolation

30   therefore fire. Do thy duty, and have thy duty,[18] for my master
    and mistress are almost frozen to death.

Curtis   There's fire ready; and therefore good Grumio the
  news.

Grumio Why "Jack boy, ho boy,"[19] and as much news as thou
35   wilt.

Curtis   Come, you are so full of cony-catching.[20]

Grumio Why therefore fire, for I have caught extreme cold.
    Where's the cook? Is supper ready, the house trimmed, rushes
    strewed,[21] cobwebs swept, the servingmen in their new
40   fustian,[22] their white stockings, and every officer[23] his
    wedding garment on? Be the Jacks fair within, the Jills fair
    without, and carpets laid, and everything in order?

Curtis   All ready. And therefore I pray thee news.

Grumio First know[24] my horse is tired, my master and mistress
45   fallen out.[25]

Curtis   How?

Grumio Out of their saddles into the dirt, and thereby hangs a
    tale.

Curtis   Let's ha't[26] good Grumio.

50 *Grumio* Lend thine ear.

Curtis   Here.

Grumio *(striking him)* There.

---

18 do thy duty, and have thy duty = do your job and keep your job
19 the first words of a then-popular song
20 deceit, knavery
21 rushes strewed = reeds spread on the floor
22 cloth made of cotton and flax
23 employee, functionary
24 let me tell you
25 fallen out = quarreled
26 have it

Curtis   This 'tis to feel a tale, not to hear a tale.

Grumio   And therefore 'tis called a sensible[27] tale. And this cuff
was but to knock at your ear, and beseech listening. Now I   55
begin, Imprimis,[28] we came down a foul hill, my master
riding behind my mistress –

Curtis   Both of[29] one horse?

Grumio   What's that to thee?

Curtis   Why, a horse.   60

Grumio   Tell thou[30] the tale. But hadst thou not crossed me,
thou shouldst have heard how her horse fell, and she under
her horse. Thou shouldst have heard in how miry[31] a place,
how she was bemoiled,[32] how he left her with the horse
upon her, how he beat me because her horse stumbled, how   65
she waded through the dirt to pluck him off me. How he
swore, how she prayed, that never prayed before. How I cried,
how the horses ran away, how her bridle was burst.[33] How I
lost my crupper, with many things of worthy[34] memory,
which now shall die in oblivion, and thou return   70
unexperienced[35] to thy grave.

Curtis   By this reckoning[36] he is more shrew than she.

Grumio   Ay; and that thou and the proudest[37] of you all shall

27 (1) physically perceptible, (2) reasonable, judicious★
28 in the first place
29 on
30 you tell
31 swampy, muddy
32 covered with dirt and muck
33 ruptured, torn
34 valuable
35 return unexperienced = retire uninformed
36 enumeration, listing
37 haughtiest, most arrogant

find when he comes home. But what talk I of this? Call forth
75 Nathaniel, Joseph, Nicholas, Philip, Walter, Sugarsop, and the
rest. Let their heads be slickly combed, their blue[38] coats
brushed, and their garters of an indifferent knit, let them
curtsy with their left legs,[39] and not presume to touch a hair
of my master's horse-tail,[40] till they kiss their[41] hands. Are
80 they all ready?

Curtis They are.

Grumio Call them forth.

Curtis Do you hear ho? You must meet my master to
countenance[42] my mistress.

85 Grumio Why she hath a face of her own.

Curtis Who knows not that?

Grumio Thou it seems, that calls for company[43] to
countenance[44] her.

Curtis I call them forth to credit[45] her.

ENTER SERVANTS

90 Grumio Why she comes to borrow[46] nothing of them.

Nathaniel Welcome home Grumio.

Philip How now, Grumio.

---

38 the color regularly worn by servants
39 with their left legs = indicating submissiveness; to put the right leg forward
    meant defiance
40 my master's horse-tail = the tail of my master's horse
41 (?) (1) the master's and the mistress's hands, or (2) their own hands, in what
    was considered an extremely deferential gesture
42 honor
43 the group/band of servants
44 Curtis means "countenance" as a verb; Grumio plays on its meaning as a
    noun, which is "face" as well as "appearance, bearing"★
45 do honor/give credit to
46 again, he deliberately takes "credit" as a noun rather than a verb

Joseph	What, Grumio.
Nicholas	Fellow Grumio.
Nathaniel	How now, old lad. 95
Grumio	(*to each in turn*) Welcome you. How now you. What you. Fellow you. And thus much for greeting. Now my spruce[47] companions, is all ready, and all things neat?
Nathaniel	All things is ready, how near is our master?
Grumio	E'en at hand, alighted[48] by this.[49] And therefore be 100 not − Cock's[50] passion, silence, I hear my master.

ENTER PETRUCHIO AND KATE

Petruchio	Where be these knaves? What, no man at door To hold my stirrup nor to take my horse? Where is Nathaniel, Gregory, Philip?
All Servants	Here, here sir, here sir. 105
Petruchio	Here sir, here sir, here sir, here sir! You logger-headed[51] and unpolished[52] grooms! What? no attendance?[53] no regard?[54] no duty? Where is the foolish knave I sent before?
Grumio	Here sir, as foolish as I was before. 110
Petruchio	You peasant swain, you whoreson malt-horse drudge![55]

47 dapper, trim
48 dismounted
49 this time
50 God's, Christ's
51 thick-headed, stupid
52 uncultured, unrefined, imperfect, rude
53 service, waiting upon
54 attention, care
55 whoreson malt-horse drudge = bastard / wretched / vile heavy / plodding slave

Did I not bid thee meet me in the park,[56]
And bring along these rascal knaves with thee?
Grumio   Nathaniel's coat sir was not fully made,[57]
115   And Gabriel's pumps[58] were all unpinked[59] i' the heel.
There was no link[60] to color Peter's hat,
And Walter's dagger was not come from sheathing.[61]
There were none fine, but Adam, Rafe, and Gregory;
The rest were ragged, old, and beggarly;
120   Yet as they are, here are they come to meet you.
Petruchio   Go rascals, go and fetch my supper in.

EXEUNT SOME OF THE SERVANTS

(*singing*) "Where is the life that late I led?
Where are those —"[62]
Sit down Kate, and welcome. Food, food, food, food![63]

ENTER SERVANTS WITH SUPPER

125   Why when I say — Nay good sweet Kate, be merry. —
Off with my boots, you rogues! You villains, when?
(*singing*) "It was the friar of orders grey,
As he forth walked on his way"[64] —

56 enclosed land around a house
57 sewn
58 slipper-like shoes
59 un-embossed (suggesting incompletion? wear and tear?)
60 blacking
61 having a sheath made for and fitted to it
62 a ballad, now lost, representing a newly married man lamenting his vanished
   freedom
63 the Folio: soud; most editors emend
64 sentimental ballad, celebrating love between a friar and a nun: see Thomas
   Percy, *Reliques of Ancient English Poetry,* 3 vols [1765] (London: Routledge /
   Thoemmes Press, 1996), 1:242–246

(*to Servant*) Out, you rogue! You pluck my foot awry:[65]

PETRUCHIO STRIKES HIM

Take that, and mend the plucking off the other. –   130
Be merry, Kate. – Some water here. What ho!

ENTER SERVANT WITH JUG OF WATER

Where's my spaniel Troilus?[66] Sirrah, get you hence
And bid my cousin Ferdinand[67] come hither.
One, Kate, that you must kiss and be acquainted with.
Where are my slippers? Shall I have some water?   135
Come Kate and wash, and welcome heartily.

SERVANT DROPS JUG, PETRUCHIO STRIKES HIM

You whoreson villain, will you let it fall?
Kate   Patience I pray you, 'twas a fault[68] unwilling.
Petruchio A whoreson beetle-headed[69] flap-eared knave!
Come Kate, sit down, I know you have a stomach.[70]   140
Will you give thanks,[71] sweet Kate, or else shall I? –
What's this? Mutton?
Servant   Ay.
Petruchio Who brought it?
Peter   I.   145
Petruchio 'Tis burnt, and so is all the meat.

---

65 pluck my foot awry = pull my foot to one side / crookedly
66 Trojan prince, Hector's brother
67 the only mention of him; he never appears and probably, to the servants'
    knowledge, did not exist
68 misdeed, offense
69 stupid
70 (1) appetite, (2) haughtiness, stubbornness, anger
71 say grace

What dogs are these! Where is the rascal cook?
How durst you villains bring it from the dresser,[72]
And serve it thus to me that love it not?

HE THROWS FOOD AND UTENSILS

150   There, take it to you,[73] trenchers,[74] cups, and all.
     You heedless joltheads[75] and unmannered[76] slaves!
     What, do you grumble? I'll be[77] with you straight.
   Kate   I pray you husband, be not so disquiet,[78]
     The meat was well, if you were so contented.[79]
155   *Petruchio*   I tell thee Kate, 'twas burnt and dried away,
     And I expressly[80] am forbid to touch it.
     For it engenders choler,[81] planteth[82] anger,
     And better 'twere that both of us did fast,
     Since of ourselves,[83] ourselves[84] are choleric,
160   Than feed it with such over-roasted flesh.
     Be patient, tomorrow 't shall be mended,
     And for this night we'll fast for company.[85]
     Come, I will bring thee to thy bridal chamber.

72 sideboard
73 take it to you = take it all away
74 wooden platters, used as plates
75 heedless joltheads = careless blockheads
76 rude, mannerless
77 be ready for you, for disciplinary purposes
78 disturbed
79 willing, satisfied
80 distinctly, absolutely
81 engenders choler = produces / creates / begets irascibility / irritability
82 deposits, inserts
83 of ourselves = by nature, naturally
84 we
85 for company = together

EXEUNT PETRUCHIO, KATE, AND CURTIS

Nathaniel Peter, didst ever see the like?

Peter   He kills her in her own humor.   165

ENTER CURTIS

Grumio Where is he?

Curtis In her chamber, making a sermon of continency[86] to
her,
And rails, and swears, and rates, that she (poor soul)
Knows not which way to stand, to look, to speak,
And sits as one new risen from a dream.   170
Away, away, for he is coming hither.

EXEUNT

ENTER PETRUCHIO

Petruchio Thus have I politicly[87] begun my reign,[88]
And 'tis my hope to end successfully.
My falcon now is sharp,[89] and passing empty.
And till she stoop,[90] she must not be full-gorged,[91]   175
For then she never looks[92] upon her lure.[93]
Another way I have to man my haggard,[94]

---

86 (1) self-restraint, moderation, (2) celibacy
87 craftily, artfully
88 kingdom, dominance
89 (1) eager, (2) hungry
90 (1) descend from the heights, swiftly, like a swooping hawk, (2) bend, bow
91 full-fed
92 will never look
93 feathered decoy, used to recall falcons
94 man my haggard = manage/rule/tame my (1) wild adult, female hawk,
   (2) hag, witch

To make her come, and know her keeper's call.

That is, to watch her, as we watch these kites[95]

180　That bate and beat,[96] and will not be obedient.

She eat[97] no meat today, nor none shall eat.

Last night she slept not, nor tonight she shall not.

As with the meat, some undeservèd[98] fault

I'll find about the making of the bed,

185　And here I'll fling the pillow, there the bolster,[99]

This way the coverlet,[100] another way the sheets.

Ay, and amid this hurly[101] I intend[102]

That all is done in reverend[103] care of her,

And in conclusion, she shall watch[104] all night,

190　And if she chance to nod, I'll rail and brawl,[105]

And with the clamor keep her still[106] awake.

This is a way to kill a wife with kindness,

And thus I'll curb[107] her mad and headstrong humor.

He that knows better how to tame a shrew,

195　Now let him speak, 'tis charity[108] to shew.[109]

EXIT

95 hawks, falcons, and other birds of prey
96 bate and beat = flutter away from the falconer, beating their wings
97 ate (pronounced ET)
98 unreasonable
99 long, stuffed cushion/pillow
100 quilt
101 commotion, uproar
102 pretend, claim
103 deeply respectful
104 be awake
105 squabble, argue, scold
106 (1) yet, (2) always
107 restrain, check
108 love of our fellow men
109 (show) set forth, demonstrate

SCENE 2

In front of Baptista's house

ENTER TRANIO AND HORTENSIO

Tranio   Is 't possible friend Litio, that Mistress Bianca
      Doth fancy any other but Lucentio?
      I tell you sir, she bears me fair in hand.[1]
Hortensio Sir, to satisfy you in[2] what I have said,
      Stand by, and mark the manner of his teaching.   5

THEY STAND ASIDE

ENTER BIANCA AND LUCENTIO

Lucentio Now mistress, profit you in[3] what you read?
Bianca   What master, read[4] you? First resolve[5] me that.
Lucentio I read that I profess,[6] the Art to Love.[7]
Bianca   And may you prove, sir, master of your art.
Lucentio While you, sweet dear, prove mistress of my heart.   10

BIANCA AND LUCENTIO MOVE TO THE SIDE OF THE STAGE

Hortensio Quick proceeders,[8] marry. Now tell me, I pray,
      You that durst swear that your Mistress Bianca
      Loved none in the world so well as Lucentio.
Tranio   O despiteful[9] love, unconstant womankind,

---

1 (?) (1) definitely favors me, or (2) clearly deceives me / leads me on
2 satisfy you in = give you proof of
3 profit you in = are you benefiting from
4 (1) think, understand, (2) expound, declare, teach
5 answer, solve
6 that I profess = that which I affirm / believe in
7 Ovid's Ars Amatoria, "Treatise on Love"
8 quick proceeders = they make rapid progress
9 spiteful, cruel, malicious, contemptuous

15   I tell thee Litio, this is wonderful.[10]

Hortensio   Mistake no more, I am not Litio,

     Nor a musician as I seem to be,

     But one that scorn to live in this disguise

     For such a one[11] as leaves a gentleman,

20   And makes a god of such a cullion.[12]

     Know sir, that I am called Hortensio.

Tranio   Signior Hortensio, I have often heard

     Of your entire[13] affection to[14] Bianca,

     And since mine eyes are witness of her lightness,[15]

25   I will with you, if you be so contented,

     Forswear[16] Bianca and her love for ever.

Hortensio   See how they kiss and court![17] Signior Lucentio,

     Here is my hand, and here I firmly vow

     Never to woo her more, but do forswear her,

30   As one unworthy all the former favors

     That I have fondly[18] flattered her withal.

Tranio   And here I take the like unfeignèd[19] oath,

     Never to marry with her though she would entreat.

     Fie on her, see how beastly[20] she doth court him!

35   *Hortensio*   Would all the world but he had quite forsworn.[21]

---

10 (1) astonishing, (2) magnificent
11 person (Bianca)
12 vile fellow, rascal
13 thorough, full
14 for
15 frivolity, fickleness, levity
16 abandon, renounce
17 woo ("make out")
18 (1) foolishly, and (2) affectionately
19 genuine, not pretended
20 offensively, exceedingly
21 "I wish everyone else in the world, except for him, had given up on her"

For me, that I may surely keep mine oath,
I will be married to a wealthy widow
Ere three days pass, which[22] hath as long loved me
As I have loved this proud disdainful haggard.
And so farewell, Signior Lucentio.   40
Kindness[23] in women, not their beauteous looks,
Shall win my love. And so I take my leave,
In resolution[24] as I swore before.

EXIT HORTENSIO

LUCENTIO AND BIANCA COME FORWARD AGAIN

Tranio   Mistress Bianca, bless you with such grace
As 'longeth to a lover's blessèd case.[25]   45
Nay, I have ta'en you napping,[26] gentle love,
And have forsworn you with Hortensio.
Bianca   Tranio, you jest. But have you both forsworn me?
Tranio   Mistress, we have.
Lucentio   Then we are rid of Litio.
Tranio   I' faith he'll have a lusty widow now,   50
That shall be wooed and wedded in a day.
Bianca   God give him joy.
Tranio   Ay, and he'll tame her.
Bianca   He says so, Tranio.
Tranio   Faith, he is gone unto the taming school.

(because Hortensio still believes that the real Lucentio is only the poor
Cambio he has disguised himself to seem?)
22 one who
23 goodwill, kind actions
24 decision, determination, firmness
25 fortune
26 ta'en you napping = caught you (1) cheating, (2) sleeping ("unaware")

55 *Bianca*   The taming school. What, is there such a place?

Tranio   Ay mistress, and Petruchio is the master,[27]

That teacheth tricks eleven and twenty long,[28]

To tame a shrew and charm her chattering tongue.

ENTER BIONDELLO

Biondello O master, master, I have watched so long

60   That I am dog-weary, but at last I spied

An ancient angel[29] coming down the hill

Will[30] serve the turn.

Tranio   What is he, Biondello?

Biondello Master, a mercatante[31] or a pedant,

I know not what, but formal[32] in apparel,

65   In gait and countenance surely like a father.

Lucentio And what of[33] him, Tranio?

Tranio   If he be credulous[34] and trust my tale,

I'll make him glad to seem Vincentio

And give assurance to Baptista Minola,

70   As if he were the right Vincentio.

Take in[35] your love, and then let me[36] alone.

EXEUNT LUCENTIO AND BIANCA

27 schoolmaster, teacher
28 eleven and twenty long: see 1.2.n22
29 (?) (1) a divine messenger? (2) an old gold coin, perhaps signifying social status?
30 who will
31 the Folio: marcantant = tradesman, merchant (MERkaTANtey)
32 proper
33 about
34 disposed to believe ("naive")
35 take in = take her inside the house
36 let me = let me be

ENTER A PEDANT

Pedant God save you sir.

Tranio   And you sir, you are welcome.
　Travel you far on, or are you at the farthest?

Pedant Sir, at the farthest[37] for a week or two,
　But then up farther,[38] and as far as Rome,   75
　And so to Tripoli,[39] if God lend me life.

Tranio What countryman, I pray?

Pedant   Of Mantua.

Tranio Of Mantua sir? Marry God forbid,
　And come to Padua careless of your life.

Pedant My life, sir? How, I pray? For that goes hard.[40]   80

Tranio 'Tis death for any one in Mantua
　To come to Padua. Know you not the cause?
　Your ships are stayed[41] at Venice, and the Duke
　For private[42] quarrel 'twixt your Duke and him,
　Hath published and proclaimed[43] it openly.   85
　'Tis marvel, but[44] that you are but newly come,
　You might have heard it else[45] proclaimed about.

Pedant Alas sir, it is worse for me than so,
　For I have bills for money by exchange[46]

37 longest
38 up farther = on further
39 in N Africa
40 goes hard = is severe / harsh
41 held, detained
42 personal
43 published and proclaimed = publicly declared and announced
44 except
45 otherwise
46 bills for money by exchange = commercial documents very like modern
　 bank checks

90   From Florence, and must here deliver them.[47]

Tranio   Well sir, to do you courtesy,
      This will I do, and this I will advise you.
      First tell me, have you ever been at Pisa?

Pedant   Ay sir, in Pisa have I often been,
95   Pisa renownèd for grave citizens.

Tranio   Among them know you one Vincentio?

Pedant   I know him not, but I have heard of him,
      A merchant of incomparable[48] wealth.

Tranio   He is my father sir, and, sooth to say,
100   In countenance somewhat doth resemble you.

Biondello (aside) As much as an apple doth an oyster, and all
      one.[49]

Tranio   To save your life in this extremity,[50]
      This favor will I do you for his sake,
      And think it not the worst of all your fortunes
105   That you are like to[51] Sir Vincentio.
      His name and credit[52] shall you undertake,[53]
      And in my house you shall be friendly[54] lodged.
      Look that you take upon you[55] as you should.
      You understand me sir. So shall you stay
110   Till you have done your business in the city.
      If this be courtesy sir, accept of it.

47 deliver them = present ("cash") them
48 matchless
49 all one = one and the same, quite the same
50 extreme need ("emergency")
51 like to = resemble
52 reputation
53 take upon yourself
54 amicably
55 take upon you = handle/comport yourself

Pedant O sir I do, and will repute[56] you ever
    The patron[57] of my life and liberty.
Tranio Then go with me, to make the matter good.[58]
    This by the way I let you understand,   115
    My father is here looked for every day
    To pass[59] assurance of a dower in marriage
    'Twixt me, and one Baptista's daughter here.
    In all these circumstances I'll instruct you.
    Go with me to clothe you as becomes you.   120

EXEUNT

56 consider, think, esteem
57 protector
58 make the matter good = perform / carry out the business
59 proceed with, get through, complete

SCENE 3

Petruchio's house

ENTER KATE AND GRUMIO

Grumio No, no forsooth, I dare not for my life.

Kate   The more my wrong, the more his spite appears.

What, did he marry me to famish me?

Beggars that come unto my father's door

5   Upon entreaty[1] have a present alms,[2]

If not, elsewhere they meet with charity.

But I, who never knew how to entreat,

Nor never needed that I should entreat,

Am starved for meat, giddy[3] for lack of sleep,

10   With oaths kept waking, and with brawling fed.

And that which spites me more than all these wants,

He does it under name[4] of perfect love.

As who should say, if I should sleep or eat

'Twere deadly sickness, or else present death.

15   I prithee go and get me some repast,[5]

I care not what, so it be wholesome food.

Grumio What say you to a neat's[6] foot?

Kate   'Tis passing good, I prithee let me have it.

Grumio I fear it is too choleric a meat.

20   How say you to a fat tripe[7] finely broiled?

---

1 earnest request, solicitation, supplication
2 present alms = immediate charity
3 dizzy★
4 the name
5 food and drink, a meal
6 ox's
7 ox or cow stomach

Kate   I like it well, good Grumio, fetch it me.

Grumio I cannot tell, I fear 'tis choleric.

 What say you to a piece of beef and mustard?

Kate   A dish that I do love to feed upon.

Grumio Ay, but the mustard is too hot a little.   25

Kate   Why then the beef, and let the mustard rest.[8]

Grumio Nay, then I will not. You shall[9] have the mustard,

 Or else you get no beef of Grumio.

Kate   Then both, or one, or anything thou wilt.

Grumio Why then the mustard without the beef.   30

Kate   Go get thee gone, thou false deluding slave,

 (*beating him*) That feed'st me with the very[10] name of meat.

 Sorrow on thee and all the pack of you

 That triumph[11] thus upon my misery!

 Go get thee gone, I say.   35

ENTER PETRUCHIO, WITH MEAT, AND HORTENSIO

Petruchio How fares my Kate? What sweeting, all amort?[12]

Hortensio Mistress, what cheer?

Kate   Faith, as cold as can be.

Petruchio Pluck up thy spirit, look cheerfully upon me.

 Here love, thou seest how diligent[13] I am,

 To dress[14] thy meat myself, and bring it thee.   40

HE SETS THE DISH ON A TABLE

 8 be left off
 9 must
10 mere
11 celebrate
12 dejected, spiritless
13 attentive
14 prepare

I am sure sweet Kate, this kindness merits thanks.

What, not a word? Nay then, thou lov'st it not,

And all my pains is sorted to no proof.[15]

(*to Servant*) Here, take away this dish.

Kate   I pray you let it stand.[16]

45   *Petruchio* The poorest service is repaid with thanks,

And so shall mine before you touch the meat.

Kate   I thank you sir.

Hortensio Signior Petruchio, fie, you are to blame.

(*sitting at the table with her*) Come Mistress Kate, I'll bear you

company.

50   *Petruchio* (*aside*) Eat it up all Hortensio, if thou lovest me.

Much good do it unto thy gentle heart.

Kate, eat apace.[17] And now, my honey love,

Will we return unto thy father's house,

And revel it as bravely[18] as the best,

55   With silken coats and caps, and golden rings,

With ruffs[19] and cuffs, and farthingales,[20] and things.

With scarfs,[21] and fans, and double change of bravery,[22]

With amber bracelets, beads, and all this knavery.[23]

What, hast thou dined? The tailor stays thy leisure,[24]

60   To deck thy body with his ruffling treasure.

---

15 sorted to no proof = obtained/reached no result
16 remain, stay
17 quickly
18 splendidly
19 frills (on sleeves and around the neck)
20 whalebone hoops
21 broad bands of silk, sashes
22 finery
23 tricks of dress/adornment
24 stays thy leisure = awaits your unoccupied time

ENTER TAILOR

Come tailor, let us see these ornaments.
Lay forth[25] the gown.

ENTER HABERDASHER[26]

What news with you, sir?

Haberdasher   Here is the cap your worship did bespeak.[27]

Petruchio   Why this was molded[28] on a porringer,[29]
A velvet dish. Fie, fie, 'tis lewd[30] and filthy,[31]   65
Why 'tis a cockle[32] or a walnut shell,
A knack,[33] a toy,[34] a trick,[35] a baby's cap.
Away with it, come let me have a bigger.

Kate   I'll have no bigger, this doth fit the time,[36]
And gentlewomen wear such caps as these.   70

Petruchio   When you are gentle, you shall have one too,
And not till then.

Hortensio   (*aside*) That will not be in haste.

Kate   Why sir, I trust I may have leave to speak,
And speak I will. I am no child, no babe.
Your betters[37] have endured me say my mind,   75

25 lay forth = let's see, display, set out
26 maker of/dealer in hats and caps
27 order
28 shaped, cut
29 small porridge bowl, often for children
30 artless, bungling, vulgar
31 disgraceful, obscene
32 mollusk, oyster
33 trinket, trifle
34 rubbish
35 sham, joke
36 fit the time = is in the current fashion
37 superiors

And if you cannot, best you stop your ears.

My tongue will tell the anger of my heart,

Or else my heart concealing it will break,

And rather than it shall, I will be free

80   Even to the uttermost[38] as I please in words.

Petruchio Why thou say'st true, it is a paltry[39] cap,

A custard-coffin,[40] a bauble,[41] a silken pie,[42]

I love thee well in that thou lik'st it not.

Kate   Love me, or love me not, I like the cap,

85   And it I will have, or I will have none.

EXIT HABERDASHER

Petruchio Thy gown?[43] Why, ay. Come tailor, let us see't.

O mercy God, what masquing[44] stuff is here?

What's this? A sleeve? 'Tis like a demi-cannon.[45]

What, up and down carved[46] like an apple tart?

90   Here's snip, and nip, and cut, and slish[47] and slash,

Like to a censer[48] in a barber's shop.

Why, what a' devil's name, tailor, call'st thou this?

Hortensio (*aside*) I see she's like to have neither cap nor gown.

Tailor   You bid me make it orderly and well,

95   According to the fashion and the time.

38 extreme
39 contemptible, despicable, worthless
40 custard crust
41 gewgaw, trifle★
42 silken pie = meat pie made of silk
43 dress
44 (1) masquerading, (2) theatricals, masques
45 large gun, with 6.5-inch bore
46 cut, sculptured
47 making a slit
48 like to a censer = looking like (?) an incense/perfumer/fumigator★

Petruchio Marry and did.[49] But if you be remembered,
    I did not bid you mar[50] it to the time.
    Go hop me[51] over every kennel[52] home,
    For you shall hop without my custom,[53] sir.
    I'll none of it. Hence, make your best of it.   100

Kate   I never saw a better fashioned[54] gown,
    More quaint,[55] more pleasing, nor more commendable.[56]
    Belike you mean to make a puppet[57] of me.

Petruchio Why true, he means to make a puppet of thee.

Tailor   She says your worship means to make a puppet of her. 105

Petruchio O monstrous arrogance, thou liest, thou thread, thou
    thimble,
    Thou yard, three-quarters, half-yard, quarter, nail![58]
    Thou flea, thou nit,[59] thou winter-cricket thou!
    Braved in mine own house with a skein[60] of thread!
    Away thou rag, thou quantity, thou remnant,   110
    Or I shall so be-mete[61] thee with thy yard[62]
    As thou shalt think on prating[63] whilst thou liv'st.
    I tell thee, I, that thou hast marred her gown.

49 I did
50 spoil, damage
51 go hop me = go hop
52 street drain, gutter
53 business, patronage
54 made
55 skillful, beautiful, fine
56 praiseworthy
57 doll, dress-up doll
58 nail's breadth (a small measure, 1 / 16 yard))
59 louse
60 with a skein = by a reel (SKANE)
61 measure
62 yardstick
63 shalt think on prating = (1) will have to think about/before chattering, or (2)
    recall/remember what happened to you, today, when you chattered

Tailor	Your worship is deceived,[64] the gown is made

115 Just as my master had direction.[65]

Grumio gave order how it should be done.

Grumio I gave him no order,[66] I gave him the stuff.[67]

Tailor But how did you desire it should be made?

Grumio Marry sir, with needle and thread.

120 *Tailor* But did you not request to have it cut?[68]

Grumio Thou hast faced[69] many things.

Tailor I have.

Grumio Face not me. Thou hast braved many men. Brave not
me, I will neither be faced nor braved. I say unto thee, I bid
125 thy master cut out the gown, but I did not bid him cut it to
pieces. Ergo,[70] thou liest.

Tailor Why, here is the note of the fashion[71] to testify.

Petruchio Read it.

Grumio The note[72] lies in ' throat, if he say I said so.

130 *Tailor* "Imprimis, a loose-bodied[73] gown."

Grumio Master, if ever I said loose-bodied gown, sew me in the
skirts of it, and beat me to death with a bottom[74] of brown
thread. I said a gown.

Petruchio Proceed.

---

64 mistaken
65 instructions
66 instruction
67 material
68 cut out
69 (1) confronted, (2) trimmed (cloth)
70 therefore
71 note of the fashion = document setting down the making
72 musical "note"
73 imprimis, a loose-bodied = first/in the first place, a loose fitting
74 skein, reel

Tailor	"With a small compassed[75] cape."	135
Grumio	I confess the cape.	
Tailor	"With a trunk[76] sleeve."	
Grumio	I confess two sleeves.	
Tailor	"The sleeves curiously[77] cut."	
Petruchio	Ay, there's the villainy.[78]	140

Grumio   Error i' the bill[79] sir, error i' the bill. I commanded the
sleeves should be cut out, and sewed up again, and that I'll
prove upon thee,[80] though thy little finger be armed in a
thimble.

Tailor   This is true that I say, and[81] I had thee in place[82]   145
where thou shouldst know[83] it.

Grumio   I am for thee straight.[84] Take thou the bill, give me
thy mete-yard, and spare not[85] me.

Hortensio   God-a-mercy, Grumio! Then he shall have no odds.[86]

Petruchio   Well sir, in brief the gown is not for me.   150

Grumio   You are i' the right sir, 'tis for my mistress.

Petruchio   Go, take it up unto thy master's use.

Grumio   (*to Tailor*) Villain, not for thy life! Take up[87] my
mistress' gown for thy master's use!

75 surrounding, flared
76 full, large
77 carefully, fastidiously
78 wrongdoing
79 (1) the note being read, (2) a legal charge
80 upon thee = against your body (in trial by combat)
81 if
82 (1) a place, or (2) field of battle
83 shouldst know = had/were obliged to acknowledge/admit
84 I am for thee straight = let's fight right now
85 spare not = don't be merciful to
86 favorable terms, chance
87 take up = raise, lift (bawdy)

155 *Petruchio* Why sir, what's your conceit in that?

Grumio O sir, the conceit[88] is deeper than you think for.

Take up my mistress' gown to his master's use!

O fie, fie, fie!

Petruchio (*aside*) Hortensio, say thou wilt see the tailor paid.

160 (*to Tailor*) Go take it hence, be gone, and say no more.

Hortensio (*aside*) Tailor, I'll pay thee for thy gown tomorrow,

Take no unkindness of[89] his hasty words.

Away I say, commend me to thy master.

EXIT TAILOR

Petruchio Well, come, my Kate, we will[90] unto your father's

165 Even in these honest mean habiliments.[91]

Our purses shall be proud,[92] our garments poor.

For 'tis the mind that makes the body rich.

And as the sun breaks through the darkest clouds,

So honor peereth[93] in the meanest habit.

170 What, is the jay more precious than the lark

Because his feathers are more beautiful?

Or is the adder better than the eel,

Because his painted[94] skin contents the eye?

O no, good Kate. Neither art thou the worse

175 For this poor furniture, and mean array.[95]

---

88 process of conception / conceiving (bawdy)
89 take no unkindness of = don't be angry / offended by
90 will go
91 clothes (haBIliMENTS)
92 honorable
93 can be seen, shows itself
94 variegated color
95 outfit, clothing

If thou account'st[96] it shame, lay it on me,
And therefore frolic.[97] We will hence forthwith,
To feast and sport us at thy father's house.
(*to Grumio*) Go call my men, and let us straight to him,
And bring our horses unto Long-lane end,   180
There will we mount, and thither walk on foot.
Let's see, I think 'tis now some[98] seven o'clock,
And well we may come there by dinner[99] time.

Kate   I dare assure you sir, 'tis almost two,
And 'twill be supper[100] time ere you come there.   185

Petruchio It shall be seven ere I go to horse.
Look what[101] I speak, or do, or think to do,
You are still crossing it. (*to Servants*) Sirs, let 't alone,
I will not go today, and ere I do,
It shall be what o'clock I say it is.   190

Hortensio (*aside*) Why, so[102] this gallant will[103] command the
sun.

EXEUNT

96 account'st = reckon/consider it
97 be merry
98 about, roughly
99 large midday meal
100 late afternoon meal
101 look what = pay attention to whatever
102 thus, in this manner
103 (1) wishes, (2) will (future tense)

SCENE 4

In front of Baptista's house

ENTER TRANIO, AND PEDANT, DRESSED AS VINCENTIO

Tranio   Sir, this is the house, please it you that I call?

Pedant   Ay what else? And, but I be deceived,

    Signior Baptista may remember me

    Near twenty years ago in Genoa,

5   Where we were lodgers at the Pegasus.[1]

Tranio   'Tis well, and hold your own,[2] in any case,

    With such austerity[3] as 'longeth to a father.

Pedant   I warrant you. But sir, here comes your boy,

    'Twere good he[4] were schooled.[5]

ENTER BIONDELLO

10   Tranio   Fear you not him. Sirrah Biondello,

    Now do your duty throughly,[6] I advise you.

    Imagine[7] 'twere the right[8] Vincentio.

Biondello   Tut, fear not me.

Tranio   But hast thou done thy errand to Baptista?

15   Biondello   I told him that your father was at Venice,

    And that you looked for him this day in Padua.

---

1 common name for an inn (the "reminiscence" is surely as fictional as the role being played)
2 hold your own = keep up/maintain/preserve your part/role
3 rigor, strictness, authority
4 that/if he
5 taught, instructed
6 thoroughly
7 think, suppose
8 true, real

Tranio Thou'rt a tall[9] fellow, hold thee that[10] to drink.
Here comes Baptista. (*to Pedant*) Set[11] your countenance[12] sir.

ENTER BAPTISTA AND LUCENTIO

Signior Baptista, you are happily met.
(*to Pedant*) Sir, this is the gentleman I told you of,   20
I pray you stand good father to me now,
Give me Bianca for my patrimony.
Pedant Soft, son.
Sir by your leave, having come to Padua
To gather in[13] some debts, my son Lucentio   25
Made me acquainted with a weighty cause
Of love between your daughter and himself.
And for the good report I hear of you,
And for the love he beareth to your daughter,
And she to him, to stay[14] him not too long,   30
I am content, in a good father's care
To have him matched, and if you please to like
No worse than I, upon[15] some agreement
Me shall you find ready and willing
With one[16] consent to have her so bestowed.   35
For curious[17] I cannot be with you,
Signior Baptista, of whom I hear so well.

 9 proper, fine
10 hold thee that = take/keep that (money given as a tip)
11 prepare, ready
12 COUNTnance
13 gather in = collect
14 delay, check
15 after, on, with
16 unified
17 difficult, fastidious

Baptista Sir, pardon me in what I have to say,
　　　　Your plainness and your shortness[18] please me well.
40　　　Right true it is your son Lucentio here
　　　　Doth love my daughter, and she loveth him,
　　　　Or both dissemble deeply their affections.
　　　　And therefore if you say no more than this,
　　　　That like a father you will deal with him,
45　　　And pass[19] my daughter a sufficient dower,
　　　　The match is made, and all is done,
　　　　Your son shall have my daughter with consent.

Tranio　I thank you, sir. Where then do you know best[20]
　　　　We be affied,[21] and such assurance ta'en[22]
50　　　As shall with either part's[23] agreement stand.[24]

Baptista Not in my house, Lucentio, for you know
　　　　Pitchers have ears, and I have many servants.
　　　　Besides, old Gremio is heark'ning still,[25]
　　　　And happily we might be interrupted.

55　*Tranio*　Then at my lodging, an it like you,
　　　　There doth my father lie.[26] And there this night,
　　　　We'll pass the business privately and well.
　　　　Send for your daughter by your servant here,

18 brevity
19 convey / transfer to
20 where then do you know best = you know best, then, where (i.e., an
　　affirmation, not a question)
21 bethrothed, engaged (afFIED)
22 assurance ta'en = written documents prepared
23 either part's = both parties'
24 firmly settle, confirm
25 heark'ning still = always listening
26 sleep, lodge

My boy shall fetch the scrivener[27] presently.
The worst is this, that at so slender warning   60
You are like to have a thin and slender pittance.[28]

Baptista   It likes me well. Cambio, hie[29] you home,
And bid Bianca make her ready straight.
And if you will,[30] tell what hath happened,
Lucentio's father is arrived in Padua,   65
And how she's like to be Lucentio's wife.

Lucentio   I pray the gods she may, with all my heart.

Tranio   Dally[31] not with the gods, but get thee gone.
Signior Baptista, shall I lead the way?
Welcome, one mess[32] is like to be your cheer.   70
Come sir, we will better it in Pisa.

Baptista   I follow you.

EXEUNT TRANIO, PEDANT, AND BAPTISTA

Biondello   Cambio.

Lucentio   What say'st thou, Biondello?

Biondello   You saw my master wink and laugh upon you?   75

Lucentio   Biondello, what of that?

Biondello   Faith nothing. But has[33] left me here behind to
expound[34] the meaning or moral of his signs and tokens.

Lucentio   I pray thee moralize[35] them.

---

27 copyist, notary (John Milton's father, a scrivener, was in effect a lawyer)
28 thin and slender pittance = a poor and scanty meal
29 hurry
30 wish
31 loiter, linger, trifle
32 portion of food
33 he has
34 interpret, explain (often used for Scripture commentary)
35 explain the moral meaning

80 *Biondello* Then thus: Baptista is safe,[36] talking with the
deceiving father of a deceitful son.

Lucentio And what of him?

Biondello His daughter is to be brought by you to the supper.

Lucentio And then?

85 *Biondello* The old priest at Saint Luke's church is at your
command at all hours.

Lucentio And what of all this?

Biondello I cannot tell, except they are busied about a
counterfeit[37] assurance. Take your assurance of her, *cum*
90 *privilegio ad imprimendum solum*.[38] To the church take the
priest, clerk, and some sufficient honest witnesses.
If this be not that you look for, I have no more to say,
But bid Bianca farewell for ever and a day.

BIONDELLO STARTS TO LEAVE

Lucentio Hear'st thou, Biondello?

95 *Biondello* I cannot tarry. I knew a wench married in an
afternoon as she went to the garden for parsley to stuff a
rabbit, and so may you sir. And so adieu sir. My master hath
appointed me to go to Saint Luke's to bid the priest be ready
to come against you come with your appendix.[39]

---

36 out of harm's way, not likely to cause trouble
37 spurious, fake★
38 "with privilege of exclusive printing" (not the strict meaning, but
so understood as an old formula granting copyright to a printer/
publisher); there is a bawdy Latinate pun in *ad imprimendum*,
"pressing on"
39 attachment

EXIT

Lucentio   I may and will, if she be so contented.   100
  She will be pleased, then wherefore should I doubt?
  Hap what hap may, I'll roundly go about[40] her.
  It shall go hard if Cambio go without her.

EXIT

40 roundly go about = go directly after

SCENE 5

The road to Padua

ENTER PETRUCHIO, KATE, HORTENSIO, AND SERVANTS

Petruchio Come on, i' God's name, once more toward our
    father's.
    Good Lord, how bright and goodly shines the moon!
Kate   The moon? The sun. It is not moonlight now.
Petruchio I say it is the moon that shines so bright.
5   *Kate*   I know it is the sun that shines so bright.
Petruchio Now by my mother's son, and that's myself,
    It shall be moon, or star, or what I list,
    Or ere[1] I journey to your father's house.
    (*to Servants*) Go on and fetch our horses back again.
10   Evermore crossed and crossed, nothing but crossed!
Hortensio Say as he says, or we shall never go.
Kate   Forward I pray, since we have come so far,
    And be[2] it moon, or sun, or what you please.
    And if you please to call it a rush candle,[3]
15   Henceforth I vow it shall be so for me.
Petruchio I say it is the moon.
Kate   I know it is the moon.
Petruchio Nay then you lie. It is the blessèd sun.
Kate   Then God be blessed, it is the blessèd sun,
20   But sun it is not, when you say it is not,
    And the moon changes even as your mind.

1 or ere = before
2 let it be
3 weak candle: a rush/reed dipped in tallow/grease (used by the poor)

What you will have it named, even that it is,
And so it shall be so for Katherine.

Hortensio (*aside*) Petruchio, go thy ways,[4] the field is won.

Petruchio Well, forward, forward! Thus the bowl should run,   25
And not unluckily against the bias.[5]
But soft, company is coming here.

ENTER VINCENTIO

(*to Vincentio*) Good morrow, gentle mistress, where away?
Tell me, sweet Kate, and tell me truly too,
Hast thou beheld a fresher[6] gentlewoman?   30
Such war[7] of white and red within[8] her cheeks!
What stars do spangle[9] heaven with such beauty,
As those two eyes become that heavenly face?
Fair lovely maid, once more good day to thee.
Sweet Kate, embrace her for her beauty's sake.   35

Hortensio (*aside*) 'A will make[10] the man mad, to make the
woman[11] of him.

Kate   Young budding virgin, fair and fresh and sweet,
Whither away, or where is thy abode?
Happy the parents of so fair a child,

---

4 go thy ways = that's it/well done/go on
5 against the bias = obliquely, in a slant (from the game of "bowls"), and thus contrary to its natural tendency
6 more blooming/youthful/energetic
7 conflict, contest
8 in
9 decorate, adorn, dot
10 'A will make = he will drive
11 make the woman = to produce/bring about/turn/transform him into a woman

40   Happier the man whom favorable stars
         Allot[12] thee for his lovely bedfellow.

       Petruchio Why how now, Kate, I hope thou art not mad,
         This is a man, old, wrinkled, faded, withered,
         And not a maiden, as thou sayst he is.

45   *Kate*   Pardon old father my mistaking eyes,
         That have been so bedazzled with the sun
         That everything I look on seemeth green.[13]
         Now I perceive thou art a reverend[14] father.
         Pardon I pray thee for my mad mistaking.

50 *Petruchio* Do, good old grandsire, and withal make known
         Which way thou travelest. If along with us,
         We shall be joyful of thy company.

       Vincentio Fair sir, and you my merry[15] mistress,
         That with your strange encounter[16] much amazed me.
55   My name is called Vincentio, my dwelling Pisa,
         And bound I am to Padua, there to visit
         A son of mine, which long I have not seen.

       Petruchio What is his name?

       Vincentio Lucentio, gentle sir.

60 *Petruchio* Happily met, the happier for thy son.
         And now by law, as well as reverend age,
         I may entitle thee my loving father.
         The sister to my wife, this gentlewoman,
         Thy son by this[17] hath married. Wonder not,

12 destine, appoint
13 (i.e., young, growing)
14 deserving of respect
15 (1) pleasant, (2) jesting, facetious, (3) animated
16 (1) greeting, address, (2) behavior
17 by this = by now/this time

Nor be not grieved, she is of good esteem,   65
Her dowry wealthy,[18] and of worthy[19] birth.
Beside,[20] so qualified[21] as may beseem[22]
The spouse of any noble gentleman.
Let me embrace with old Vincentio,
And wander[23] we to see thy honest son,   70
Who will of thy arrival be full joyous.

Vincentio But is this true? Or is it else your pleasure,
Like pleasant travelers, to break[24] a jest
Upon the company you overtake?

Hortensio I do assure thee, father, so it is.   75

Petruchio Come go along and see the truth hereof,
For our first merriment hath made thee jealous.[25]

EXEUNT ALL BUT HORTENSIO

Hortensio Well Petruchio, this has put me in heart.[26]
Have to[27] my widow! And if she be froward,
Then hast thou taught Hortensio to be untoward.[28]   80

EXIT

18 opulent, luxurious, copious
19 excellent
20 in addition
21 accomplished
22 suit (verb)
23 travel
24 crack, utter ("crack a joke")
25 suspicious
26 put me in heart = given me courage / spirit
27 have to = here's to
28 difficult to manage / unruly / perverse / stubborn

Act 5

𝕰

In front of Lucentio's house

ENTER BIONDELLO, LUCENTIO, AND BIANCA ON ONE SIDE,
GREMIO ON THE OTHER

Biondello Softly and swiftly sir, for the priest is ready.
Lucentio I fly, Biondello. But they may chance to need thee at
home, therefore leave us.
Biondello Nay faith, I'll see the church o' your back,[1] and then
5   come back to my mistress as soon as I can.

EXEUNT LUCENTIO, BIANCA, AND BIONDELLO

Gremio   I marvel Cambio comes not all this while.

ENTER PETRUCHIO, KATE, VINCENTIO, AND ATTENDANTS

Petruchio Sir here's the door, this is Lucentio's house.
My father's bears[2] more toward the marketplace,

---

1 o' your back = at your back ("from behind you")
2 takes/leads me

Thither must I, and here I leave you sir.

Vincentio You shall not choose but drink before you go, 10
  I think I shall command[3] your welcome here,
  And by all likelihood some cheer is toward.[4]

HE KNOCKS

Gremio They're busy within, you were best knock louder.

PEDANT APPEARS ABOVE, AT A WINDOW

Pedant What's he that knocks as[5] he would beat down the
  gate? 15

Vincentio Is Signior Lucentio within, sir?

Pedant He's within sir, but not to be spoken withal.[6]

Vincentio What if a man bring him a hundred pound or two to
  make merry withal?

Pedant Keep your hundred pounds to yourself, he shall need 20
  none so long as I live.

Petruchio (*to Vincentio*) Nay, I told you your son was well beloved
  in Padua. (*to Pedant*) Do you hear, sir? To leave frivolous
  circumstances,[7] I pray you tell Signior Lucentio that his
  father is come from Pisa, and is here at the door to speak with 25
  him.

Pedant Thou liest. His father is come from Padua, and here
  looking out at the window.

Vincentio Art thou his father?

Pedant Ay sir, so his mother says, if I may believe her. 30

---

3 shall command = must insist on
4 in progress (toWARD)
5 as if
6 with
7 leave frivolous circumstances = to put aside trifling/unimportant matters

Petruchio *(to Vincentio)* Why, how now, gentleman. Why this is flat
    knavery to take upon you another man's name.

Pedant   Lay hands on[8] the villain, I believe 'a means to cozen
    somebody in this city under my countenance.[9]

ENTER BIONDELLO

35   Biondello *(aside)* I have seen them in the church together, God
    send 'em good shipping.[10] But who is here? Mine old master,
    Vincentio! Now we are undone[11] and brought to nothing.[12]

Vincentio *(seeing Biondello)* Come hither, crack-hemp.[13]

Biondello I hope I may choose, sir.

40   Vincentio Come hither, you rogue. What, have you forgot me?

Biondello Forgot you, no sir. I could not forget you, for I never
    saw you before in all my life.

Vincentio What, you notorious[14] villain! Didst thou never see
    thy master's father, Vincentio?

45   Biondello What, my old worshipful[15] old master? Yes marry sir,
    see where he looks out of the window.

Vincentio Is't so, indeed?

HE BEATS BIONDELLO

---

8 lay hands on = seize
9 under my countenance = by pretending to be me
10 sailing, a good voyage ("good fortune")
11 ruined
12 brought to nothing = everything is finished / destroyed
13 crack-hemp = someone likely to strain a hempen rope by being hanged
   ("rascal")
14 famous, obvious
15 distinguished, honorable

Biondello Help, help, help, here's a madman will[16] murder me.

EXIT BIONDELLO

Pedant   Help, son! Help, Signior Baptista!

PEDANT DISAPPEARS FROM THE WINDOW

Petruchio Prithee, Kate, let's stand aside and see the end of this   50
controversy.

THEY STEP TO THE SIDE

ENTER PEDANT, BAPTISTA, TRANIO, AND SERVANTS

Tranio   Sir, what are you that offer[17] to beat my servant?

Vincentio What am I sir! Nay, what are you sir? Q immortal
gods! O fine[18] villain! A silken doublet, a velvet hose,[19] a
scarlet cloak, and a copatain[20] hat! O I am undone, I am   55
undone! While I play[21] the good husband at home, my son
and my servant spend all at the university.

Tranio   How now, what's the matter?

Baptista   What, is the man lunatic?

Tranio   Sir, you seem a sober ancient gentleman by your habit,   60
but your words show you a madman. Why sir, what 'cerns[22]
it you if I wear pearl and gold? I thank my good father, I am
able to maintain it.

Vincentio Thy father! O villain, he is a sailmaker in Bergamo.

16 who wants to
17 intend, try
18 consummate, absolute, perfect
19 breeches
20 high-crowned ("sugar-loaf")
21 am busily engaged / working hard at
22 concerns

65 *Baptista*   You mistake sir, you mistake sir. Pray, what do you
think is his name?

Vincentio   His name, as if I knew not his name. I have brought
him up ever since he was three years old, and his name is
Tranio.

70 *Pedant*   Away, away, mad ass, his name is Lucentio, and he is
mine only son and heir to the lands of me, Signior Vincentio.

Vincentio   Lucentio! O he hath murdered his master! Lay hold
on[23] him, I charge you in the Duke's name. O my son, my
son! Tell me thou villain, where is my son, Lucentio?

75 *Tranio*   Call forth[24] an officer.

ENTER OFFICER

Carry[25] this mad knave to the jail. Father Baptista, I charge
you see that he be forthcoming.[26]

Vincentio   Carry me to the jail!

Gremio   Stay officer, he shall not go to prison.

80 *Baptista*   Talk not, Signior Gremio. I say he shall[27] go to prison.

Gremio   Take heed, Signior Baptista, lest you be cony-
catched[28] in this business. I dare swear[29] this is the right
Vincentio.

Pedant   Swear if thou darest.

85 *Gremio*   Nay, I dare not swear it.[30]

Tranio   Then thou wert best say that I am not Lucentio.

---

23 lay hold on = seize
24 call forth = summon
25 convey, bring
26 kept in safe custody
27 (1) will, (2) must
28 fooled, duped, swindled
29 dare swear = affirm, declare
30 (1) No, I don't dare swear it, or (2) No, I don't dare not to swear it (Tranio's
next words strongly suggest that the second alternative is correct)

Gremio Yes, I know thee to be Signior Lucentio.

Baptista Away with the dotard,[31] to the jail with him!

Vincentio Thus strangers may be hailed[32] and abused. (*to Tranio*)
 O monstrous villain!   90

  ENTER BIONDELLO, LUCENTIO, AND BIANCA

Biondello O we are spoiled,[33] and yonder he is. (*to Lucentio*)
 Deny him, forswear him, or else we are all undone.

Lucentio (*kneeling*) Pardon, sweet father.

Vincentio   Lives my sweet son?

  BIONDELLO, TRANIO, AND PEDANT RUN OUT

Bianca (*kneeling*) Pardon, dear father.

Baptista   (*to Bianca*) How hast
 thou offended?
 Where is Lucentio?

Lucentio   Here's Lucentio,   95
 Right son to the right Vincentio,
 That have by marriage made thy daughter mine,
 While counterfeit supposes[34] bleared thine eyne.[35]

Gremio Here's packing,[36] with a witness,[37] to deceive us all.

Vincentio Where is that damnèd villain Tranio,   100
 That faced and braved me in this matter so?

Baptista Why, tell me is not this my Cambio?

Bianca Cambio is changed into Lucentio.

31 old/senile imbecile
32 greeted, welcomed
33 destroyed
34 fakes
35 bleared thine eyne = dimmed your eyes
36 plotting, defrauding
37 with a witness = and that's a fact, without a doubt

Lucentio   Love wrought[38] these miracles. Bianca's love
105   Made me exchange my state with Tranio,
         While he did bear my countenance in the town.
         And happily I have arrived at the last[39]
         Unto the wishèd haven[40] of my bliss.
         What Tranio did, myself enforced him to.
110   Then pardon him, sweet father, for my sake.

Vincentio   I'll slit the villain's nose that would have sent me to the
         jail.

Baptista   (*to Lucentio*) But do you hear sir? Have you married
         my daughter without asking my good will?

115 *Vincentio*   Fear not Baptista, we[41] will content you, go to.[42] But I
         will in,[43] to be revenged for this villainy.

EXIT VINCENTIO

Baptista   And I[44] to sound[45] the depth of this knavery.

EXIT BAPTISTA

Lucentio   Look not pale, Bianca, thy father will not frown.[46]

EXEUNT LUCENTIO AND BIANCA

Gremio   My cake is dough,[47] but I'll in[48] among the rest,

38 worked
39 at the last = at last, finally
40 harbor
41 (?) the royal "we," meaning "I"?
42 come on (exclamation)
43 I will in = I will go in the house
44 I will go in
45 penetrate, inquire into
46 disapprove
47 my cake is dough = I have failed (proverbial)
48 go in

Out of hope of all but my share of the feast. 120

EXIT GREMIO

PETRUCHIO AND KATE COME FORWARD

Kate   Husband, let's follow to see the end of this ado.[49]

Petruchio First kiss me, Kate, and we will.

Kate   What, in the midst of the street?

Petruchio What, art thou ashamed of me?

Kate   No sir, God forbid, but ashamed to kiss. 125

Petruchio Why then let's home again. (*to Grumio*) Come sirrah,

    let's away.

Kate   Nay, I will give thee a kiss.

SHE KISSES HIM

                      Now pray thee love, stay.

Petruchio Is not this well? Come, my sweet Kate.

    Better once than never, for never too late.

EXEUNT

49 fuss, commotion

SCENE 2

Lucentio's house

ENTER BAPTISTA, VINCENTIO, GREMIO, PEDANT,
LUCENTIO, BIANCA, PETRUCHIO, KATE, HORTENSIO,
WIDOW, AND TRANIO, BIONDELLO, GRUMIO,
AND OTHERS, ATTENDING

Lucentio   At last,[1] though long[2], our jarring notes agree,[3]
    And time it is[4] when raging war is done
    To smile at 'scapes[5] and perils overblown.[6]
    My fair Bianca, bid my father welcome,
5   While I with self-same kindness welcome thine.
    Brother Petruchio, sister Katherina,
    And thou Hortensio, with thy loving widow,
    Feast with the best, and welcome to my house.
    My banquet is[7] to close our stomachs up,[8]
10   After our great good cheer.[9] Pray you, sit down,
    For now we sit to chat as well as eat.

THEY SEAT THEMSELVES AT TABLE

Petruchio   Nothing but sit and sit, and eat and eat!
Baptista   Padua affords[10] this kindness, son Petruchio.

1 finally, in the end
2 it has been a long time
3 come into harmony
4 time it is = it is time
5 escapes
6 that have passed away
7 is designed/meant
8 close our stomachs up = (1) fill our stomachs, and (2) put an end to/
  conclude our passionate conflicts
9 great good cheer = the larger meal eaten, earlier, to celebrate the wedding
10 grants, gives

Petruchio	Padua affords nothing but what is kind.	
Hortensio	For both our sakes I would that word were true.	15
Petruchio	Now for my life, Hortensio fears his widow.	
Widow	Then never trust me if I be afeard.[11]	
Petruchio	You are very sensible, and yet you miss my sense.	

I mean Hortensio is afeard of you.

Widow	He that is giddy thinks the world turns[12] round.	20
Petruchio	Roundly replied.	
Kate	Mistress, how mean you that?	
Widow	Thus I conceive by[13] him.	
Petruchio	Conceives by me! How likes Hortensio that?	
Hortensio	My widow says, thus she conceives her tale.	
Petruchio	Very well mended. Kiss him for that, good widow.	25
Kate	"He that is giddy thinks the world turns round,"	

I pray you tell me what you meant by that.

Widow	Your husband being troubled with a shrew,	

Measures my husband's sorrow by his woe.

And now you know my meaning. 30

Kate	A very mean meaning.	
Widow	Right, I mean you.	
Kate	And I am mean, indeed, respecting you.[14]	
Petruchio	To[15] her, Kate!	
Hortensio	To her, widow!	
Petruchio	A hundred marks,[16] my Kate does put her down.	35

11 be afeard = am frightened / afraid
12 the world turns = that it is the world which is spinning
13 conceive by = (1) imagine / think, from / because of, (2) become pregnant
   by
14 (1) in comparison to, (2) regarding
15 go at
16 gold / silver coins

Hortensio	That's my office.
Petruchio	Spoke like an officer. Ha'[17] to thee, lad.

HE DRINKS TO HORTENSIO

Baptista	How likes Gremio these quick-witted folks?
Gremio	Believe me sir, they butt[18] together well.

40 *Bianca* Head and butt.[19] An hasty-witted body[20]
Would say your head and butt were head and horn.[21]

Vincentio Ay mistress bride, hath that awakened you?

Bianca Ay, but not frighted me. Therefore I'll sleep again.

Petruchio Nay that you shall not, since you have begun.

45 Have at you[22] for a better jest or two.

Bianca Am I your bird?[23] I mean to shift[24] my bush,
And then[25] pursue me as you draw[26] your bow.
(*speaking to everyone, as hostess*) You are welcome all.

EXEUNT BIANCA, KATE, AND WIDOW

Petruchio She hath prevented me.[27] Here, Signior Tranio,
50 This bird you[28] aimed at, though you hit her not.
Therefore a health to all that shot and missed.

17 here's
18 bang, strike
19 tail, buttock
20 hasty-witted body = irritable / rash person
21 a cuckold's horn: the application of this is obscure
22 have at you = make an attempt
23 (secondary meanings include (1) girl, (2) prey, object of attack)
24 change
25 after that you'll have to
26 as you draw = while you're in the act of drawing
27 prevented me = forestalled / surpassed me
28 (in the guise of Lucentio)

Tranio   O sir, Lucentio slipped me[29] like his greyhound,
    Which runs himself, and catches for his master.

Petruchio A good swift simile,[30] but something currish.[31]

Tranio   'Tis well sir that you hunted for yourself.   55
    'Tis thought your deer[32] does hold you at a bay.

Baptista   O, O, Petruchio! Tranio hits[33] you now.

Lucentio   I thank thee for that gird,[34] good Tranio.

Hortensio Confess, confess, hath he not hit you here?

Petruchio A' has a little galled[35] me, I confess.   60
    And as[36] the jest did glance away from me,
    'Tis ten to one it maimed[37] you two outright.[38]

Baptista   Now in good sadness,[39] son Petruchio,
    I think thou hast the veriest shrew of all.

Petruchio Well, I say no. And therefore, for assurance,[40]   65
    Let's each one send unto his wife,
    And he whose wife is most obedient
    To come at first when he doth send for her,
    Shall win the wager which we will propose.

Hortensio Content. What's the wager?

Lucentio   Twenty crowns.   70

29 slipped me = eased me out of / freed me from my collar (as one frees a dog to
   let it run)
30 swift simile = quick(-witted) comparison (SImiLEE)
31 something currish = a bit ignoble
32 deer / dear: a hunted deer will sometimes turn and fight
33 reaches / strikes / scores against
34 (1) blow, (2) gibe, dig
35 irritated, chafed
36 then, as
37 mutilated, crippled
38 (1) completely, (2) immediately
39 good sadness = all seriousness
40 for assurance = to make sure

Petruchio   Twenty crowns?

   I'll venture[41] so much of[42] my hawk or hound,

   But twenty times so much upon my wife.

Lucentio   A hundred then.

Hortensio   Content.

Petruchio   A match, 'tis done.

Hortensio   Who shall begin?

75 *Lucentio*   That will I.

   Go Biondello, bid your mistress come to me.

Biondello   I go.

EXIT BIONDELLO

Baptista   Son, I'll be your half,[43] Bianca comes.

Lucentio   I'll have no halves. I'll bear it all myself.

ENTER BIONDELLO

   How now, what news?

80 *Biondello*   Sir, my mistress sends you word

   That she is busy, and she cannot come.

Petruchio   How? She's busy, and she cannot come.

   Is that an answer?

Gremio   Ay, and a kind one too.

   Pray God sir, your wife send you not a worse.

85 *Petruchio*   I hope better.

Hortensio   Sirrah Biondello, go and entreat my wife

   To come to me forthwith.

41 risk
42 on
43 partner ("I'll go halves with you")

EXIT BIONDELLO

Petruchio   O ho, entreat her!
   Nay then she must needs come.
Hortensio   I am afraid, sir,
   Do what you can, yours will not be entreated.

ENTER BIONDELLO

   Now, where's my wife?   90
Biondello   She says you have some goodly jest in hand,
   She will not come. She bids you come to her.
Petruchio   Worse and worse, she will not come! O vile,
   Intolerable, not to be endured![44]
   Sirrah Grumio, go to your mistress, say   95
   I command her come to me.

EXIT GRUMIO

Hortensio   I know her answer.
Petruchio   What?
Hortensio   She will not.
Petruchio   The fouler fortune[45] mine, and there an end.

ENTER KATE

Baptista   Now by my holidame,[46] here comes Katherina!
Kate   What is your will sir, that you send for me?   100
Petruchio Where is your sister, and Hortensio's wife?
Kate   They sit conferring[47] by the parlor fire.

44 inTOleREYble NOT to BE enDURED
45 luck
46 holy sanctuary/relic
47 conversing

Petruchio   Go fetch them hither. If they deny to come,

Swinge[48] me them soundly forth unto their husbands.

105   Away I say, and bring them hither straight.

EXIT KATE

Lucentio   Here is a wonder, if you talk of a wonder.

Hortensio   And so it is. I wonder what it bodes.[49]

Petruchio   Marry, peace it bodes, and love, and quiet life,

An awful[50] rule, and right[51] supremacy.

110   And to be short, what not, that's sweet and happy.[52]

Baptista   Now fair befall thee,[53] good Petruchio.

The wager thou hast won, and I will add

Unto their losses twenty thousand crowns –

Another dowry to another daughter,

115   For she is changed as[54] she had never been.

Petruchio   Nay, I will win my wager better yet,

And show more sign of her obedience,

Her new-built virtue and obedience.

See where she comes, and brings your froward wives

120   As prisoners to her womanly persuasion.

ENTER KATE WITH BIANCA AND WIDOW

Katherine, that cap of yours becomes you not,

Off with that bauble, throw it underfoot.

---

48 (1) castigate, scold, (2) whip, lash
49 (1) means, signifies, (2) portends, predicts
50 sublimely majestic / reverential
51 righteous, legitimate, proper
52 everything that's sweet and happy (literally, "what that's sweet and happy does it NOT bode")
53 fair befall thee = may good things come to you
54 as if

KATE OBEYS

Widow	Lord, let me never have a cause to sigh,
	Till I be brought to such a silly pass![55]
Bianca	Fie, what a foolish duty call you this?
Lucentio	I would your duty were as foolish too.
	The wisdom[56] of your duty, fair Bianca,
	Hath cost me a hundred crowns since supper time.
Bianca	The more fool you for laying on my duty.
Petruchio	Katherine, I charge thee tell[57] these headstrong women
	What duty they do owe their lords and husbands.
Widow	Come, come, you're mocking. We will have no telling.
Petruchio	Come on I say, and first begin with her.
Widow	She shall not.
Petruchio	I say she shall, and first begin with her.
Kate	Fie, fie, unknit[58] that threatening unkind brow,
	And dart not scornful glances from those eyes,
	To wound thy lord, thy king, thy governor.[59]
	It blots thy beauty, as frosts do bite the meads,[60]
	Confounds thy fame,[61] as whirlwinds shake fair buds,
	And in no sense is meet or amiable.[62]
	A woman moved is like a fountain troubled,[63]

Line numbers in margin: 125, 130, 135, 140

---

55 "Lord, may I never have any reason to sigh / Until after I am put into such a silly state" (i.e., never)
56 (non-wisdom)
57 make known to
58 smooth out
59 one who exercises authoritative control
60 bite the meads = wound/injure the meadows
61 confounds thy fame = defeats/destroys/ruins your reputation
62 AMeeAble
63 a fountain troubled = an agitated/turbid stream

Muddy, ill-seeming, thick, bereft of beauty,
And while it is so, none so dry or thirsty
145   Will deign to sip, or touch one drop of it.
Thy husband is thy lord, thy life, thy keeper,
Thy head, thy sovereign — one that cares for thee,
And for thy maintenance commits[64] his body
To painful[65] labor, both by sea and land,
150   To watch[66] the night in storms, the day in cold,
Whilst thou liest warm at home, secure and safe,
And craves no other tribute at thy hands
But love, fair looks, and true obedience —
Too little payment for so great a debt.
155   Such duty as the subject owes the prince,
Even such a woman oweth to her husband.
And when she is froward, peevish,[67] sullen, sour,
And not obedient to his honest will,
What is she but a foul contending rebel,[68]
160   And graceless traitor[69] to her loving lord?
I am ashamed that women are so simple,
To offer[70] war, where they should kneel for peace.
Or seek for rule, supremacy, and sway,[71]

64 consigns, gives
65 difficult, toilsome, irksome
66 keep vigil, be on the look out
67 spiteful, perverse
68 contending rebel = antagonistic resistor of due and proper authority (the idea of rebellion was associated with the "rebel," Satan, and thus with the word "enemy")
69 graceless traitor = ungodly / depraved / wicked / indecent betrayer (the word was then associated with Judas Iscariot, who betrayed Jesus)
70 propose
71 power

When they are bound to serve, love, and obey.
Why are our bodies soft, and weak, and smooth,   165
Unapt[72] to toil and trouble in the world,
But that our soft conditions,[73] and our hearts,
Should well agree with our external parts?
Come, come, you froward and unable worms,[74]
My mind hath been as big as one of yours,   170
My heart as great, my reason haply more,
To bandy[75] word for word, and frown for frown.
But now I see our lances are but straws,
Our strength as[76] weak, our weakness past compare,
That seeming to be most, which we indeed least are.   175
Then vail your stomachs,[77] for it is no boot,[78]
And place your hands below your husband's foot.
In token of which duty, if he please,
My hand is ready, may it do him ease.[79]

Petruchio   Why there's a wench! Come on, and kiss me Kate.   180
Lucentio   Well go thy ways, old lad, for thou shalt ha't.[80]
Vincentio   'Tis a good hearing,[81] when children are toward.
Lucentio   But a harsh hearing, when women are froward.
Petruchio   Come Kate, we'll to bed.

72 unfitted
73 natures
74 unable worms = powerless/incompetent/unqualified mere insects
   ("miserable creatures")
75 hit/toss back and forth (as a ball in tennis)
76 exactly that
77 vail your stomachs = cast down/surrender/abase your desires/appetites
78 use, profit, avail
79 comfort, gratification
80 win the prize (rhymes with "Kate")
81 good hearing = good to hear

185   We three are[82] married, but you two are sped.

'Twas I won the wager, (*to Lucentio*) though you hit the white.[83]

And being[84] a winner, God give you good night!

EXEUNT PETRUCHIO AND KATE

Hortensio Now go thy ways, thou hast tamed a curst shrew.

Lucentio   'Tis a wonder, by your leave,[85] she will[86] be tamed so.

EXEUNT

---

82 are all of us
83 (1) white target, in archery, (2) Bianca, in Italian = white
84 since I am
85 by your leave = if I may have your permission to say so
86 is willing/desires to

℘

The Taming of the Shrew begins with the very odd two scenes of the Induction, in which a noble practical joker gulls the drunken tinker, Christopher Sly, into the delusion that he is a great lord about to see a performance of Kate and Petruchio's drama. That makes their comedy, the rest of *The Taming of the Shrew*, a play-within-a-play, which does not seem at all appropriate to its representational effect upon an audience. Though skillfully written, the Induction would serve half a dozen other comedies by Shakespeare as well or as badly as it coheres with the *Shrew*. Critical ingenuity has proposed several schemes creating analogies between Christopher Sly and Petruchio, but I am one of the unpersuaded. And yet Shakespeare had some dramatic purpose in his Induction, even if we have not yet surmised it. Sly is not brought back at the conclusion of Shakespeare's *Shrew*, perhaps because his disenchantment necessarily would be cruel, and would disturb the mutual triumph of Kate and Petruchio, who rather clearly are going to be the happiest married couple in Shakespeare (short of the Macbeths, who end separately but each badly). Two points can be accepted as generally cogent about the Induction: it somewhat distances us from the performance of the *Shrew,* and it also hints that social dislocation is a form of madness. Sly, aspiring above his social station, becomes as insane as Malvolio in *Twelfth Night.*

Since Kate and Petruchio are social equals, their own disloca-tion may be their shared, quite violent forms of expression, which Petruchio "cures" in Kate at the high cost of augmenting his own boisterousness to an extreme where it hardly can be distinguished from a paranoid mania. Who cures, and who is cured, remains a disturbing matter in this marriage, which doubtless will maintain itself against a cowed world by a common front of formidable pugnacity (much more cunning in Kate than in her roaring boy of a husband). We all know one or two marriages like theirs; we can admire what works, and we resolve also to keep away from a couple so closed in upon itself, so little concerned with others or with otherness.

It may be that Shakespeare, endlessly subtle, hints at an analogy between Christopher Sly and the happily married couple, each in a dream of its own from which we will not see Sly wake, and which Kate and Petruchio need never abandon. Their final shared reality is a kind of conspiracy against the rest of us: Petruchio gets to swagger, and Kate will rule him and the household, perpetually acting her role as the reformed shrew. Several feminist critics have asserted that Kate marries Petruchio against her will, which is simply untrue. Though you have to read carefully to see it, Petru-chio is accurate when he insists that Kate fell in love with him at first sight. How could she not? Badgered into violence and ve-hemence by her dreadful father Baptista, who vastly prefers the authentic shrew, his insipid younger daughter Bianca, the high-spirited Kate desperately needs rescue. The swaggering Petruchio provokes a double reaction in her: outwardly furious, inwardly smitten. The perpetual popularity of the *Shrew* derives not from male sadism in the audience but from the sexual excitation of women and men alike.

The *Shrew* is as much a romantic comedy as it is a farce. The mutual roughness of Kate and Petruchio makes a primal appeal, and yet the humor of their relationship is highly sophisticated. The amiable ruffian Petruchio is actually an ideal—that is to say an overdetermined—choice for Kate in her quest to free herself from a household situation far more maddening than Petruchio's antic zaniness. Roaring on the outside, Petruchio is something else within, as Kate gets to see, understand, and control, with his final approval. Their rhetorical war begins as mutual sexual provocation, which Petruchio replaces, after marriage, with his hyperbolical game of childish tantrums. It is surely worth remarking that Kate, whatever her initial sufferings as to food, costume, and so on, has only one true moment of agony, when Petruchio's deliberately tardy arrival for the wedding makes her fear she has been jilted:

Baptista Signor Lucentio, this is the 'pointed day
    That Katharine and Petruchio should be married,
    And yet we hear not of our son-in-law.
    What will be said, what mockery will it be?
    To want the bridegroom when the priest attends
    To speak the ceremonial rites of marriage?
    What says Lucentio to this shame of ours?
Kate   No shame but mine, I must forsooth be forced
    To give my hand, opposed against my heart,
    Unto a mad-brain rudesby, full of spleen,
    Who wooed in haste, and means to wed at leisure.

> I told you, I, he was a frantic fool,
> Hiding his bitter jests in blunt behavior,
> And to be noted for a merry man.
> He'll woo a thousand, 'point the day of marriage,
> Make friends invited, and proclaim the banns,
> Yet never means to wed where he hath wooed.
> Now must the world point at poor Katherine,
> And say lo, there is mad Petruchio's wife —
> If it would please him come and marry her.
> *Tranio* Patience, good Katherine, and Baptista too.
> Upon my life, Petruchio means but well,
> Whatever fortune stays him from his word.
> Though he be blunt, I know him passing wise.
> Though he be merry, yet withal he's honest.
> *Kate* Would Katherine had never seen him though.

> [3.2.1–26]

No one enjoys being jilted, but this is not the anxiety of an unwilling bride. Kate, authentically in love, nevertheless is unnerved by the madcap Petruchio, lest he turn out to be an obsessive practical joker, betrothed to half of Italy. When, after the ceremony, Petruchio refuses to allow his bride to attend her own wedding feast, he crushes what she calls her "spirit to resist" with a possessive diatribe firmly founded upon the doubtless highly patriarchal Tenth Commandment:

> They shall go forward Kate, at thy command.
> Obey the bride, you that attend on her,
> Go to the feast, revel and domineer,
> Carouse full measure to her maidenhead,
> Be mad and merry, or go hang yourselves.

But for my bonny Kate, she must with me.
(*to Kate*) Nay, look not big, not stamp, nor stare, nor fret,
I will be master of what is mine own.
She is my goods, my chattels, she is my house,
My household stuff, my field, my barn,
My horse, my ox, my ass, my anything,
And here she stands, touch her whoever dare,
I'll bring mine action on the proudest he
That stops my way in Padua. Grumio,
Draw forth thy weapon, we are beset with thieves,
Rescue thy mistress if thou be a man.
(*to Kate*) Fear not, sweet wench, they shall not touch thee,
Kate,
I'll buckler thee against a million.

[3.2.214–31]

This histrionic departure, with Petruchio and Grumio bran-
dishing drawn swords, is a symbolic carrying-off, and begins
Petruchio's almost phantasmagoric "cure" of poor Kate, which
will continue until at last she discovers how to tame the swag-
gerer:

Petruchio Come on, i' God's name, once more toward our
father's.
Good Lord, how bright and goodly shines the moon!
Kate   The moon? The sun. It is not moonlight now.
Petruchio I say it is the moon that shines so bright.
Kate   I know it is the sun that shines so bright.
Petruchio Now by my mother's son, and that's myself,
It shall be moon, or star, or what I list,
Or ere I journey to your father's house.

(*to Servants*) Go on, and fetch our horses back again.

Evermore crossed and crossed; nothing but crossed.

Hortensio Say as he says, or we shall never go.

Kate Forward I pray, since we have come so far,

And be it moon, or sun, or what you please.

And if you please to call it a rush candle,

Henceforth I vow it shall be so for me.

Petruchio I say it is the moon.

Kate I know it is the moon.

Petruchio Nay then you lie. It is the blessèd sun.

Kate Then God be blessed, it is the blessèd sun.

But sun it is not, when you say it is not,

And the moon changes even as your mind.

What you will have it named, even that it is,

And so it shall be so for Katherine.

[4.5.1–22]

From this moment on, Kate firmly rules while endlessly protesting her obedience to the delighted Petruchio, a marvelous Shakespearean reversal of Petruchio's earlier strategy of proclaiming Kate's mildness even as she raged on. There is no more charming a scene of married love in all Shakespeare than this little vignette on a street in Padua:

Kate Husband, let's follow to see the end of this ado.

Petruchio First kiss me, Kate, and we will.

Kate What, in the midst of the street?

Petruchio What, art thou ashamed of me?

Kate No, sir, God forbid; but ashamed to kiss.

Petruchio Why then let's home again. (*to Grumio*) Come, sirrah, let's away.

Kate   Nay, I will give thee a kiss. Now pray thee, love, stay.
Petruchio Is not this well? Come, my sweet Kate.

　　Better once than never, for never too late.

EXEUNT

[5.1.121−29]

One would have to be tone deaf (or ideologically crazed) not to hear in this a subtly exquisite music of marriage at its happiest. I myself always begin teaching the *Shrew* with this passage, because it is a powerful antidote to all received nonsense, old and new, concerning this play. (One recent edition of the play offers extracts from English Renaissance manuals on wife beating, from which one is edified to learn that, on the whole, such exercise was not recommended. Since Kate does hit Petruchio, and he does not retaliate—though he warns her not to repeat this exuberance—it is unclear to me why wife beating is invoked at all.) Even subtler is Kate's long and famous speech, her advice to women concerning their behavior toward their husbands, just before the play concludes. Again, one would have to be very literal-minded indeed not to hear the delicious irony that is Kate's undersong, centered on the great line "I am ashamed that women are so simple." It requires a very good actress to deliver this set piece properly, and a better director than we tend to have now, if the actress is to be given her full chance, for she is advising women how to rule absolutely, while feigning obedience:

　　Fie, fie, unknit that threatening unkind brow,
　　And dart not scornful glances from those eyes,
　　To wound thy lord, thy king, thy governor.
　　It blots thy beauty, as frosts do bite the meads,

Confounds thy fame, as whirlwinds shake fair buds,
And in no sense is meet or amiable.
A woman moved is like a fountain troubled,
Muddy, ill-seeming, thick, bereft of beauty,
And while it is so, none so dry or thirsty
Will deign to sip, or touch one drop of it.
Thy husband is thy lord, thy life, thy keeper,
Thy head, thy sovereign – one that cares for thee,
And for thy maintenance commits his body
To painful labor, both by sea and land,
To watch the night in storms, the day in cold,
Whilst thou liest warm at home, secure and safe,
And craves no other tribute at thy hands
But love, fair looks, and true obedience –
Too little payment for so great a debt.
Such duty as the subject owes the prince,
Even such a woman oweth to her husband.
And when she is froward, peevish, sullen, sour,
And not obedient to his honest will,
What is she but a foul contending rebel,
And graceless traitor to her loving lord?
I am ashamed that women are so simple,
To offer war where they should kneel for peace.
Or seek for rule, supremacy, and sway,
When they are bound to serve, love, and obey.
Why are our bodies soft, and weak, and smooth,
Unapt to toil and trouble in the world,
But that our soft conditions, and our hearts,
Should well agree with our external parts?
Come, come, you froward and unable worms,

My mind hath been as big as one of yours,
My heart as great, my reason haply more,
To bandy word for word and frown for frown.
But now I see our lances are but straws,
Our strength as weak, our weakness past compare,
That seeming to be most, which we indeed least are.
Then vail your stomachs, for it is no boot,
And place your hands below your husband's foot.
In token of which duty, if he please,
My hand is ready, may it do him ease.

[5.2.136–79]

I have quoted this complete precisely because its redundancy and hyperbolical submissiveness are critical to its nature as a secret language or code now fully shared by Kate and Petruchio. "True obedience" here is considerably less sincere than it purports to be, or even if sexual politics are to be invoked, it is as immemorial as the Garden of Eden. "Strength" and "weakness" interchange their meanings, as Kate teaches not ostensible subservience but the art of her own will, a will considerably more refined than it was at the play's start. The speech's meaning explodes into Petruchio's delighted (and overdetermined) response: "Why, there's a wench! Come on, and kiss me, Kate."

If you want to hear this line as the culmination of a "problem play," then perhaps you yourself are the problem. Kate does not need to be schooled in "consciousness raising." Shakespeare, who clearly preferred his women characters to his men (always except-ing Falstaff and Hamlet), enlarges the human, from the start, by subtly suggesting that women have the truer sense of reality.

FURTHER READING

This is not a bibliography, but a selective set of starting places.

Texts

Holderness, Graham, and Bryan Loughrey, eds. *A Pleasant Conceited Historie, Called The Taming of a Shrew*. New York: Harvest Wheatsheaf, 1992.

Shakespeare. *The First Folio of Shakespeare.* 2d ed. Prepared by Charlton Hinman, with a new Introduction by Peter W. M. Blayney. New York: Norton, 1996.

Language

Houston, John Porter. *The Rhetoric of Poetry in the Renaissance and Seventeenth Century*. Baton Rouge: Louisiana State University Press, 1983.

———. *Shakespearean Sentences: A Study in Style and Syntax*. Baton Rouge: Louisiana State University Press, 1988.

Kermode, Frank. *Shakespeare's Language.* New York: Farrar, Straus and Giroux, 2000.

Kökeritz, Helge. *Shakespeare's Pronunciation*. New Haven: Yale University Press, 1953.

Lanham, Richard A. *The Motives of Eloquence: Literary Rhetoric in the Renaissance*. New Haven and London: Yale University Press, 1976.

Marcus, Leah S. *Unediting the Renaissance: Shakespeare, Marlowe, Milton.* London: Routledge, 1996.

The Oxford English Dictionary: Second Edition on CD-ROM, version 3.0. New York: Oxford University Press, 2002.

Raffel, Burton. *From Stress to Stress: An Autobiography of English Prosody.* Hamden, Conn.: Archon Books, 1992.

Ronberg, Gert. *A Way with Words: The Language of English Renaissance Literature.* London: Arnold, 1992.

Trousdale, Marion. *Shakespeare and the Rhetoricians.* Chapel Hill: University of North Carolina Press, 1982.

Culture

Bindoff, S. T. *Tudor England.* Baltimore: Penguin, 1950.

Bradbrook, M. C. *Shakespeare: The Poet in His World.* New York: Columbia University Press, 1978.

Brown, Cedric C., ed. *Patronage, Politics, and Literary Tradition in England, 1558–1658.* Detroit, Mich.: Wayne State University Press, 1993.

Buxton, John. *Elizabethan Taste.* London: Harvester, 1963.

Cowan, Alexander. *Urban Europe, 1500–1700.* New York: Oxford University Press, 1998.

Finucci, Valeria, and Regina Schwartz, eds. *Desire in the Renaissance: Psychoanalysis and Literature.* Princeton, N.J.: Princeton University Press, 1994.

Fumerton, Patricia, and Simon Hunt, eds. *Renaissance Culture and the Everyday.* Philadelphia: University of Pennsylvania Press, 1999.

Halliday, F. E. *Shakespeare in His Age.* South Brunswick, N.J.: Yoseloff, 1965.

Harrison, G. B., ed. *The Elizabethan Journals: Being a Record of Those Things Most Talked of During the Years 1591–1597.* Abridged ed. 2 vols. New York: Doubleday Anchor, 1965.

Harrison, William. *The Description of England: The Classic Contemporary [1577] Account of Tudor Social Life.* Edited by Georges Edelen. Ithaca, N.Y.: Cornell University Press for the Folger Shakespeare Library, 1968. 2d ed., New York: Dover, 1994.

Jardine, Lisa. *Reading Shakespeare Historically*. London: Routledge, 1996.
———. *Worldly Goods: A New History of the Renaissance*. London: Macmillan, 1996.

Jeanneret, Michel. *A Feast of Words: Banquets and Table Talk in the Renaissance*. Translated by Jeremy Whiteley and Emma Hughes. Chicago: University of Chicago Press, 1991.

Lockyer, Roger. *Tudor and Stuart Britain*. London: Longmans, 1964.

Rose, Mary Beth, ed. *Renaissance Drama as Cultural History: Essays from Renaissance Drama, 1977–1987*. Evanston, Ill.: Northwestern University Press, 1990.

Tillyard, E. M. W. *The Elizabethan World Picture*. London: Chatto and Windus, 1943. Reprint, Harmondsworth: Penguin, 1963.

Willey, Basil. *The Seventeenth-Century Background: Studies in the Thought of the Age in Relation to Poetry and Religion*. New York: Columbia University Press, 1933. Reprint, New York: Doubleday, 1955.

Wilson, F. P. *The Plague in Shakespeare's London*. 2d ed. Oxford: Oxford University Press, 1963.

Wilson, John Dover. *Life in Shakespeare's England: A Book of Elizabethan Prose*. 2d ed. Cambridge: Cambridge University Press, 1913. Reprint, Harmondsworth: Penguin, 1944.

Zimmerman, Susan, and Ronald F. E. Weissman, eds. *Urban Life in the Renaissance*. Newark: University of Delaware Press, 1989.

Dramatic Development

Cohen, Walter. *Drama of a Nation: Public Theater in Renaissance England and Spain*. Ithaca, N.Y.: Cornell University Press, 1985.

Dessen, Alan C. *Shakespeare and the Late Moral Plays*. Lincoln: University of Nebraska Press, 1986.

Fraser, Russell A., and Norman Rabkin, eds. *Drama of the English Renaissance*. 2 vols. Upper Saddle River, N.J.: Prentice Hall, 1976.

Happé, Peter, ed. *Tudor Interludes*. Harmondsworth: Penguin, 1972.

Laroque, François. *Shakespeare's Festive World: Elizabethan Seasonal Entertainment and the Professional Stage*. Translated by Janet Lloyd. Cambridge: Cambridge University Press, 1991.

Norland, Howard B. *Drama in Early Tudor Britain, 1485–1558.* Lincoln: University of Nebraska Press, 1995.

Theater and Stage

Doran, Madeleine. *Endeavors of Art: A Study of Form in Elizabethan Drama.* Milwaukee: University of Wisconsin Press, 1954.

Gurr, Andrew. *Playgoing in Shakespeare's London.* Cambridge: Cambridge University Press, 1987.

————. *The Shakespearian Stage, 1574–1642.* 3d ed. Cambridge: Cambridge University Press, 1992.

Harrison, G. B. *Elizabethan Plays and Players.* Ann Arbor: University of Michigan Press, 1956.

Holmes, Martin. *Shakespeare and His Players.* New York: Scribner, 1972.

Ingram, William. *The Business of Playing: The Beginnings of the Adult Professional Theater in Elizabethan London.* Ithaca, N.Y.: Cornell University Press, 1992.

Salgado, Gamini. *Eyewitnesses of Shakespeare: First Hand Accounts of Performances, 1590–1890.* New York: Barnes and Noble, 1975.

Thomson, Peter. *Shakespeare's Professional Career.* Cambridge: Cambridge University Press, 1992.

Weimann, Robert. *Shakespeare and the Popular Tradition in the Theater: Studies in the Social Dimension of Dramatic Form and Function.* Edited by Robert Schwartz. Baltimore: Johns Hopkins University Press, 1978.

Yachnin, Paul. *Stage-Wrights: Shakespeare, Jonson, Middleton, and the Making of Theatrical Value.* Philadelphia: University of Pennsylvania Press, 1997.

Biography

Halliday, F. E. *The Life of Shakespeare.* Rev. ed. London, Duckworth, 1964.

Honigmann, F. A. J. *Shakespeare: The "Lost Years."* 2d ed. Manchester: Manchester University Press, 1998.

Schoenbaum, Samuel. *Shakespeare's Lives.* New ed. Oxford: Clarendon Press, 1991.

———. *William Shakespeare: A Compact Documentary Life.* Oxford: Oxford University Press, 1977.

General

Bergeron, David M., and Geraldo U. de Sousa. *Shakespeare: A Study and Research Guide.* 3d ed. Lawrence: University of Kansas Press, 1995.

Berryman, John. *Berryman's Shakespeare,* ed. John Haffenden. New York: Farrar, Straus and Giroux, 1999.

Bradbey, Anne, ed. *Shakespearian Criticism, 1919–35.* London: Oxford University Press, 1936.

Colie, Rosalie L. *Shakespeare's Living Art.* Princeton, N.J.: Princeton University Press, 1974.

Grene, David. *The Actor in History: Studies in Shakespearean Stage Poetry.* University Park: Pennsylvania State University Press, 1988.

Goddard, Harold C. *The Meaning of Shakespeare.* 2 vols. Chicago: University of Chicago Press, 1951.

Kaufmann, Ralph J. *Elizabethan Drama: Modern Essays in Criticism.* New York: Oxford University Press, 1961.

McDonald, Russ. *The Bedford Companion to Shakespeare: An Introduction with Documents.* Boston: Bedford, 1996.

Raffel, Burton. *How to Read a Poem.* New York: Meridian, 1984.

Ricks, Christopher, ed. *English Drama to 1710.* Rev. ed. Harmondsworth: Sphere, 1987.

Siegel, Paul N., ed. *His Infinite Variety: Major Shakespearean Criticism since Johnson.* Philadelphia: Lippincott, 1964.

Sweeting, Elizabeth J. *Early Tudor Criticism: Linguistic and Literary.* Oxford: Blackwell, 1940.

Van Doren, Mark. *Shakespeare.* New York: Holt, 1939.

Weiss, Theorore. *The Breath of Clowns and Kings: Shakespeare's Early Comedies and Histories.* New York: Atheneum, 1971.

Wells, Stanley, ed. *The Cambridge Companion to Shakespeare Studies.* Cambridge: Cambridge University Press, 1986.

FINDING LIST

🔊

Repeated unfamiliar words and meanings, alphabetically arranged, with act, scene, and footnote number of first occurrence, in the spelling (form) of that first occurrence

achieve	1.1.150	*bonny*	2.1.112
action	intro.1.138	*braves* (noun)	3.1.14
affable	1.2.56	*cause* (noun)	1.2.21
amazèd	2.1.87	*chafe*	1.2.104
amiss	1.2.46	*chance* (noun)	1.2.25
an	intro.1.98	*chance* (verb)	intro.1.70
ancient	intro.2.34	*charge*	intro.1.21
approved	1.1.9	*charm* (verb)	1.1.192
banquet	intro.1.51	*chat*	2.1.97
bauble	4.3.41	*cheer* (noun)	intro.2.90
beast	intro.1.44	*chide*	1.1.153
becomes	1.1.204	*common*	1.1.43
beholding	1.2.139	*confess*	1.1.144
belike	intro.1.94	*content* (verb)	1.1.85
beseech	1.2.113	*counsel*	intro.1.160
bestow	1.1.58	*countenance*	4.1.44